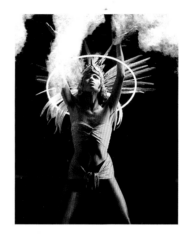

N I G H T   S H O T S

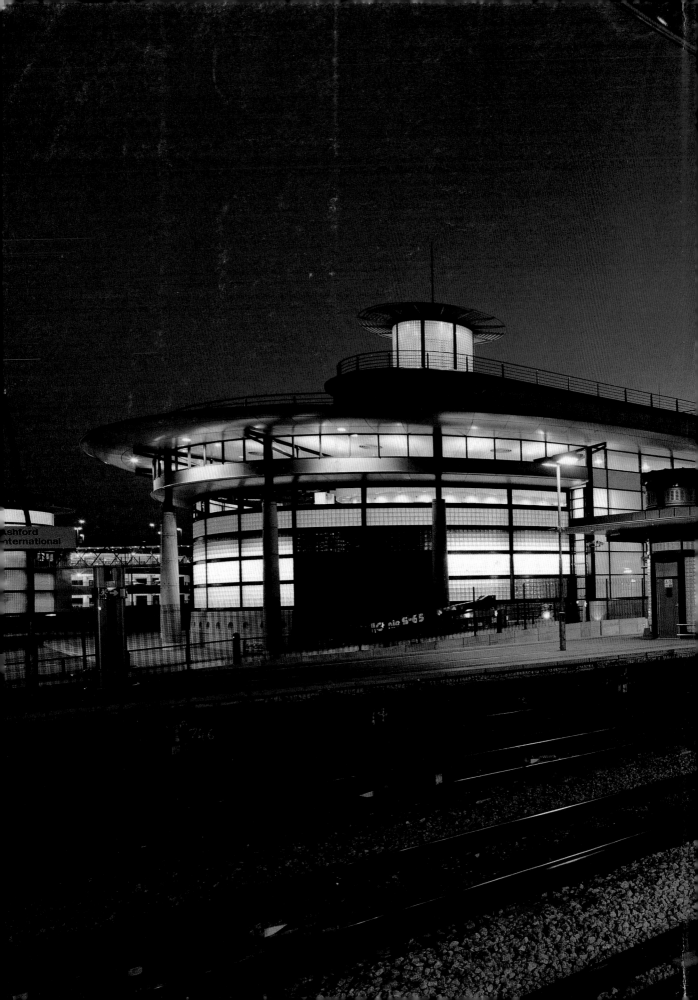

Pro·Lighting

ALEX LARG and JANE WOOD

NIGHT
SHOTS

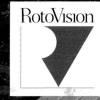

RotoVision

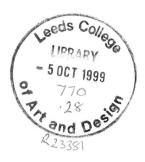

A Quintet Book

Published and distributed by
RotoVision SA
7 rue du Bugnon
1299 Crans
Switzerland

RotoVision SA Sales Office
Sheridan House
112/116A Western Road
Hove, East Sussex BN3 IDD
England
Tel: +44 1273 72 72 68
Fax: +44 1273 72 72 69

Distributed to the trade in the United States:
Watson-Guptill Publications
1515 Broadway
New York, NY 10036

ISBN 2-88046-324-6

This book was designed and produced by
Quintet Publishing Ltd
6 Blundell Street
London N7 9BH

Creative Director: Richard Dewing
Art Director: Clare Reynolds
Designer: Fiona Roberts @ The Design Revolution
Senior Editor: Anna Briffa
Editor: Bill Ireson
Picture Researchers: Alex Larg and Jane Wood

Typeset in Great Britain by
Central Southern Typesetters, Eastbourne
Printed in Singapore
Production and Separation by ProVision Pte. Ltd.
Tel: +65 334 7720
Fax: +65 334 7721

C O N T E N T S

▼

THE PRO-LIGHTING SERIES

▼

THE MOST COMMON RESPONSE FROM THE PHOTOGRAPHERS WHO CONTRIBUTED TO THIS BOOK, WHEN THE CONCEPT WAS EXPLAINED TO THEM, WAS "I'D BUY THAT". THE AIM IS SIMPLE: TO CREATE A LIBRARY OF BOOKS, ILLUSTRATED WITH FIRST-CLASS PHOTOGRAPHY FROM ALL AROUND THE WORLD, WHICH SHOW EXACTLY HOW EACH INDIVIDUAL PHOTOGRAPH IN EACH BOOK WAS LIT.

Who will find it useful? Professional photographers, obviously, who are either working in a given field or want to move into a new field. Students, too, who will find that it gives them access to a very much greater range of ideas and inspiration than even the best college can hope to present. Art directors and others in the visual arts will find it a useful reference book, both for ideas and as a means of explaining to photographers exactly what they want done. It will also help them to understand what the photographers are saying to them. And, of course, "pro/am" photographers who are on the cusp between amateur photography and earning money with their cameras will find it invaluable: it shows both the standards that are required, and the means of achieving them.

The lighting set-ups in each book vary widely, and embrace many different types of light source: electronic flash, tungsten, HMIs, and light brushes, sometimes mixed with daylight and flames and all kinds of other things. Some are very complex; others are very simple. This variety is very important, both as a source of ideas and inspiration and because each book as a whole has no axe to grind: there is no editorial bias towards one kind of lighting or another, because the pictures were chosen on the basis of impact and (occasionally) on the basis of technical difficulty. Certain subjects are, after all, notoriously difficult to light and can present a challenge even to experienced photographers. Only after the picture selection had been made was there any attempt to understand the lighting set-up.

This book is a part of the fourth series: BEAUTY SHOTS, NIGHT SHOTS, and NEW GLAMOUR. Previous titles in the series include INTERIOR SHOTS, GLAMOUR SHOTS, SPECIAL EFFECTS, NUDES, PRODUCT SHOTS, STILL LIFE, FOOD SHOTS, LINGERIE SHOTS and PORTRAITS. The intriguing thing in all of them is to see the degree of underlying similarity, and the degree of diversity, which can be found in a single discipline or genre.

Beauty shots feature beauty accessories and cosmetics for a commercial market so the lighting set-ups tend to be bright and strong to give powerful, bold images to grace the pages of many a beauty magazine or advertisement. Glamour shots, by contrast, concentrate on models, often nudes, and altogether softer lighting tends to be used, though having said that, many of the bold new-style shots are deliberately stark and provocative and the choice of harsher lighting can be used to good effect in these cases. For night shots, inevitably the use of available light without much by way of additional lighting features much more prominently than in any other book in the series.

The structure of the books is straightforward. After this initial introduction, which changes little among all the books in the series, there is a brief guide and glossary of lighting terms. Then, there is specific introduction to the individual area or areas of photography which are covered by the book. Sub-divisions of each discipline are arranged in chapters, inevitably with a degree of overlap, and each chapter has its own introduction. Finally, there is a directory of those photographers who have contributed work.

If you would like your work to be considered for inclusion in future books, please write to Quintet Publishing Ltd, 6 Blundell Street, London N7 9BH and request an Information Pack. DO NOT SEND PICTURES, either with the initial inquiry or with any subsequent correspondence, unless requested; unsolicited pictures may not always be returned. When a book is planned which corresponds with your particular area of expertise, we will contact you. Until then, we hope that you enjoy this book; that you will find it useful; and that it helps you in your work.

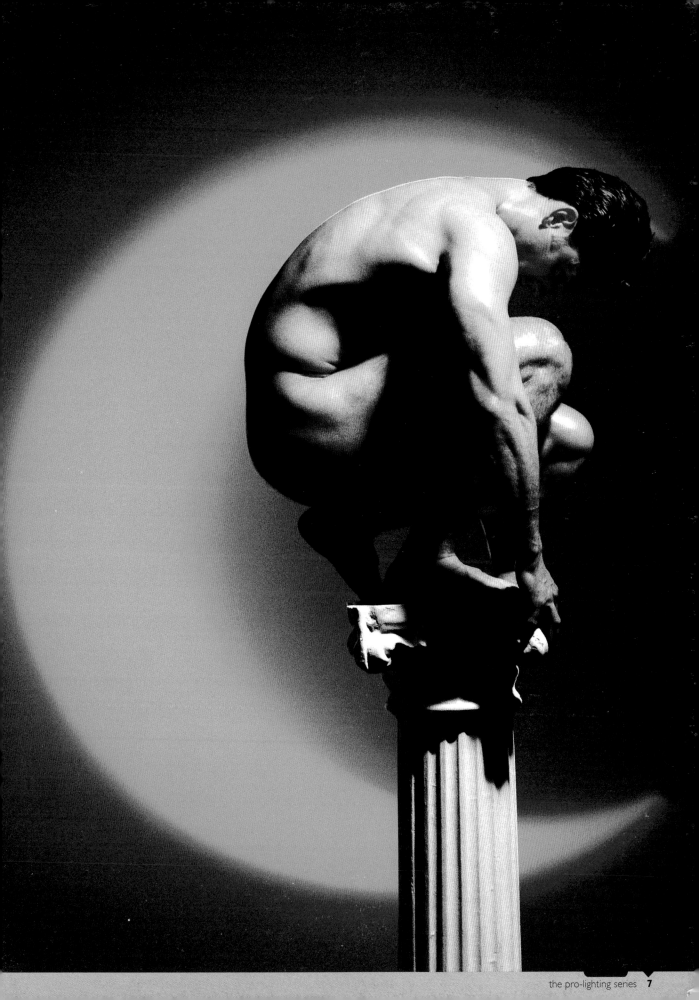

HOW TO USE THIS BOOK

▼

THE LIGHTING DRAWINGS IN THIS BOOK ARE INTENDED AS A GUIDE TO THE LIGHTING SET-UP RATHER THAN AS ABSOLUTELY ACCURATE DIAGRAMS. PART OF THIS IS DUE TO THE VARIATION IN THE PHOTOGRAPHERS' OWN DRAWINGS, SOME OF WHICH WERE MORE COMPLETE (AND MORE COMPREHENSIBLE) THAN OTHERS, BUT PART OF IT IS ALSO DUE TO THE NEED TO REPRESENT COMPLEX SET-UPS IN A WAY WHICH WOULD NOT BE NEEDLESSLY CONFUSING.

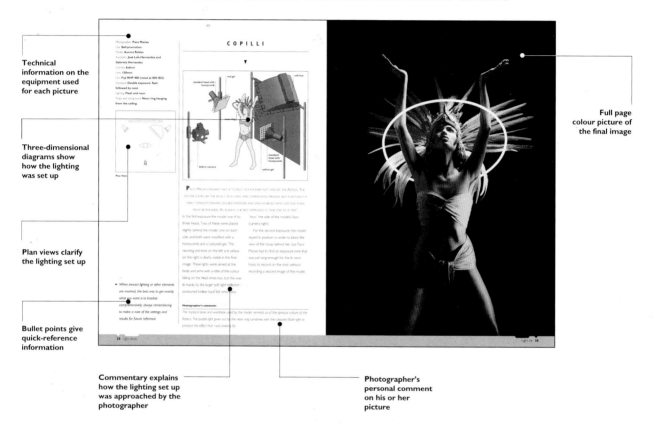

Technical information on the equipment used for each picture

Three-dimensional diagrams show how the lighting was set up

Plan views clarify the lighting set up

Bullet points give quick-reference information

Full page colour picture of the final image

Commentary explains how the lighting set up was approached by the photographer

Photographer's personal comment on his or her picture

Distances and even sizes have been compressed and expanded: and because of the vast variety of sizes of soft boxes, reflectors, bounces and the like, we have settled on a limited range of conventionalized symbols. Sometimes, too, we have reduced the size of big bounces, just to simplify the drawing.

None of this should really matter, however. After all, no photographer works strictly according to rules and preconceptions: there is always room to move this light a little to the left or right,

to move that light closer or further away, and so forth, according to the needs of the shot. Likewise, the precise power of the individual lighting heads or (more important) the lighting ratios are not always given; but again, this is something which can be "fine tuned" by any photographer wishing to reproduce the lighting set-ups in here.

We are however confident that there is more than enough information given about every single shot to merit its inclusion in the book: as well as purely

lighting techniques, there are also all kinds of hints and tips about commercial realities, photographic practicalities, and the way of the world in general.

The book can therefore be used in a number of ways. The most basic, and perhaps the most useful for the beginner, is to study all the technical information concerning a picture which he or she particularly admires, together with the lighting diagrams, and to try to duplicate that shot as far as possible with the equipment available.

A more advanced use for the book is as a problem solver for difficulties you have already encountered: a particular technique of back lighting, say, or of creating a feeling of light and space. And, of course, it can always be used simply as a source of inspiration.

The information for each picture follows the same plan, though some individual headings may be omitted if they were irrelevant or unavailable. The photographer is credited first, then the client, together with the use for which the picture was taken. Next come the other members of the team who worked on the picture: stylists, models, art directors, whoever. Camera and lens come next, followed by film. With film, we have named brands and types, because different films have very different ways of rendering colours and tonal values. Exposure comes next: where the lighting is electronic flash, only the aperture is given, as illumination is of course independent of shutter speed. Next, the lighting equipment is briefly summarized — whether tungsten or flash, and what sort of heads — and finally there is a brief note on props and backgrounds. Often, this last will be obvious from the picture, but in other cases you may be surprised at what has been pressed into service, and how different it looks from its normal role.

The most important part of the book is however the pictures themselves. By studying these, and referring to the lighting diagrams and the text as necessary, you can work out how they were done; and showing how things are done is the brief to which the *Pro Lighting* series was created.

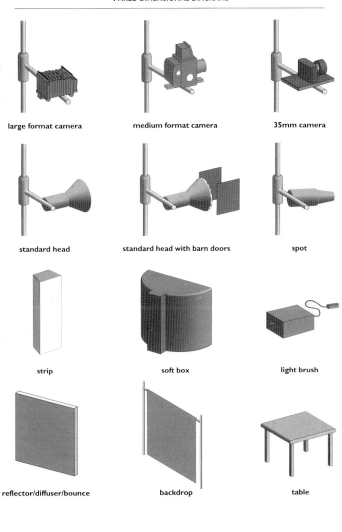

D I A G R A M   K E Y

The following is a key to the symbols used in the three-dimensional and plan view diagrams. All commonly used elements such as standard heads, reflectors etc., are listed. Any special or unusual elements involved will be shown on the relevant diagrams themselves.

THREE-DIMENSIONAL DIAGRAMS

large format camera   medium format camera   35mm camera

standard head   standard head with barn doors   spot

strip   soft box   light brush

reflector/diffuser/bounce   backdrop   table

PLAN VIEW DIAGRAMS

large format camera   medium format camera   35mm camera   bounce

standard head   standard head with barn doors   spot   gobo

diffuser

reflector

strip   soft box   light brush   backdrop   table

GLOSSARY OF LIGHTING TERMS

▼

LIGHTING, LIKE ANY OTHER CRAFT, HAS ITS OWN JARGON AND SLANG. UNFORTUNATELY, THE DIFFERENT TERMS ARE NOT VERY WELL STANDARDIZED, AND OFTEN THE SAME THING MAY BE DESCRIBED IN TWO OR MORE WAYS OR THE SAME WORD MAY BE USED TO MEAN TWO OR MORE DIFFERENT THINGS. FOR EXAMPLE, A SHEET OF BLACK CARD, WOOD, METAL OR OTHER MATERIAL WHICH IS USED TO CONTROL REFLECTIONS OR SHADOWS MAY BE CALLED A FLAG, A FRENCH FLAG, A DONKEY OR A GOBO — THOUGH SOME PEOPLE WOULD RESERVE THE TERM "GOBO" FOR A FLAG WITH HOLES IN IT, WHICH IS ALSO KNOWN AS A COOKIE. IN THIS BOOK, WE HAVE TRIED TO STANDARDIZE TERMS AS FAR AS POSSIBLE. FOR CLARITY, A GLOSSARY IS GIVEN BELOW, AND THE PREFERRED TERMS USED IN THIS BOOK ARE ASTERISKED.

Acetate
see Gel

Acrylic sheeting
Hard, shiny plastic sheeting, usually methyl methacrylate, used as a diffuser ("opal") or in a range of colours as a background.

*Barn doors
Adjustable flaps affixed to a lighting head which allow the light to be shaded from a particular part of the subject.

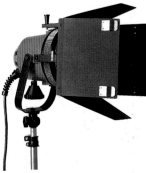

Barn doors

Boom
Extension arm allowing a light to be cantilevered out over a subject.

*Bounce
A passive reflector, typically white but also, (for example) silver or gold, from which light is bounced back onto the subject. Also used in the compound term "Black Bounce", meaning a flag used to absorb light rather than to cast a shadow.

Continuous lighting
What its name suggests: light which shines continuously instead of being a brief flash.

Contrast
see Lighting ratio

Cookie
see Gobo

*Diffuser
Translucent material used to diffuse light. Includes tracing paper, scrim, umbrellas, translucent plastics such as Perspex and Plexiglas, and more.

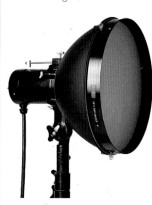

Electronic flash: standard head with parallel snoot (Strobex)

Donkey
see Gobo

Effects light
Neither key nor fill; a small light, usually a spot, used to light a particular part of the subject. A hair light on a model is an example of an effects (or "FX") light.

*Fill
Extra lights, either from a separate head or from a reflector, which "fills" the shadows and lowers the lighting ratio.

Fish fryer
A small Soft Box.

*Flag
A rigid sheet of metal, board, foam-core or other material which is used to absorb light or to create a shadow. Many flags are painted black on one side and white (or brushed silver) on the other, so that they can be used either as flags or as reflectors.

*Flat
A large Bounce, often made of a thick sheet of expanded polystyrene or foam-core (for lightness).

Foil
see Gel

French flag
see Flag

Frost
see Diffuser

*Gel
Transparent or (more rarely) translucent coloured material used to modify the colour of a light. It is an abbreviation of "gelatine (filter)", though most modern "gels" for lighting use are actually of acetate.

*Gobo
As used in this book, synonymous with "cookie": a flag with cut-outs in it, to cast interestingly-shaped shadows. Also used in projection spots.

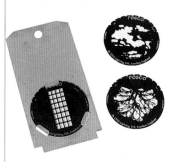

"Cookies" or "gobos" for projection spotlight (Photon Beard)

*Head
Light source, whether continuous or flash. A "standard head" is fitted with a plain reflector.

*HMI
Rapidly-pulsed and

effectively continuous light source approximating to daylight and running far cooler than tungsten. Relatively new at the time of writing, and still very expensive.

*Honeycomb

Grid of open-ended hexagonal cells, closely resembling a honeycomb. Increases directionality of

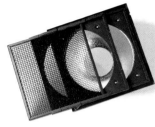

Honeycomb (Hensel)

light from any head.

Incandescent lighting

see Tungsten

Inky dinky

Small tungsten spot.

*Key or key light

The dominant or principal light, the light which casts the shadows.

Kill Spill

Large flat used to block spill.

*Light brush

Light source "piped" through fibre-optic lead. Can be used to add highlights, delete shadows and modify lighting, literally by "painting with light".

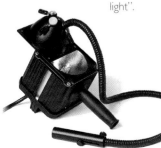

Electronic Flash: light brush "pencil" (Hensel)

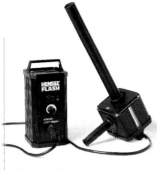

Electronic Flash: light brush "hose" (Hensel)

Lighting ratio

The ratio of the key to the fill, as measured with an incident light meter. A high lighting ratio (8:1 or above) is very contrasty, especially in colour, a low lighting ratio (4:1 or less) is flatter or softer. A 1:1 lighting ratio is completely even, all over the subject.

*Mirror

Exactly what its name suggests. The only reason for mentioning it here is that reflectors are rarely mirrors, because mirrors create "hot spots" while reflectors diffuse light. Mirrors (especially small shaving mirrors) are however widely used, almost in the same way as effects lights.

Northlight

see Soft Box

Perspex

Brand name for acrylic sheeting.

Plexiglas

Brand name for acrylic sheeting.

*Projection spot

Flash or tungsten head with projection optics for casting a clear image of a gobo or cookie. Used to create textured lighting effects and shadows.

*Reflector

Either a dish-shaped

surround to a light, or a bounce.

*Scrim

Heat-resistant fabric

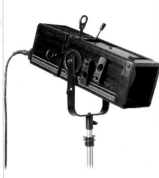

Electronic Flash: projection spotlight (Strobex)

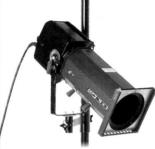

Tungsten Projection spotlight (Photon Beard)

diffuser, used to soften lighting.

*Snoot

Conical restrictor, fitting over a lighting head. The light can only escape from the small hole in the end, and is

therefore very directional.

*Soft box

Large, diffuse light source made by shining a light

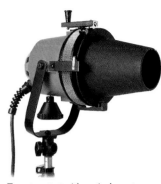

Tungsten spot with conical snoot (Photon Beard)

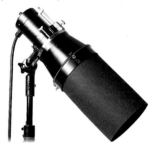

Electronic Flash: standard head with parallel snoot (Strobex)

through one or two layers of diffuser. Soft boxes come in all kinds of shapes

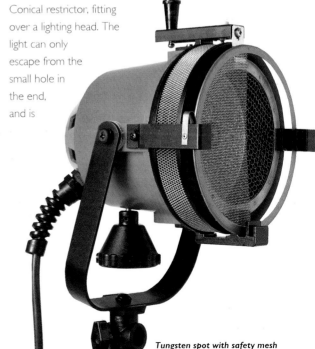

Tungsten spot with safety mesh (behind) and wire half diffuser scrim (Photon Beard)

Electronic flash: standard head with large reflector and diffuser (Strobex)

and sizes, from about 30x30cm to 120x180cm and larger. Some soft boxes are rigid; others are made of fabric stiffened with poles resembling fibreglass fishing rods. Also known as a northlight or a windowlight, though these can also be created by shining standard heads through large (120x180cm or larger) diffusers.

*Spill

Light from any source which ends up other than on the subject at which it is pointed. Spill may be used to provide fill, or to light backgrounds, or it may be controlled with flags, barn doors, gobos etc.

*Spot

Directional light source. Normally refers to a light using a focusing system

with reflectors or lenses or both, a "focusing spot", but also loosely used as a reflector head rendered more directional with a honeycomb.

*Strip or strip light

Lighting head, usually flash, which is much longer than it is wide.

Electronic flash: strip light with removable barn doors (Strobex)

Strobe

Electronic flash. Strictly, a "strobe" is a stroboscope or rapidly repeating light source, though it is also the name of a leading manufacturer.

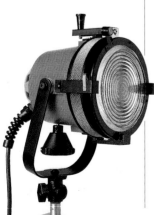

Tungsten spot with removable Fresnel lens. The knob at the bottom varies the width of the beam (Photon Beard)

Strobex, formerly Strobe Equipment.

Swimming pool

A very large Soft Box.

*Tungsten

Incandescent lighting. Photographic tungsten

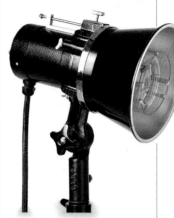

Electronic flash: standard head with standard reflector (Strobex)

lighting runs at 3200°K or 3400°K, as compared with domestic lamps which run at 2400°K to 2800°K or thereabouts.

*Umbrella

Exactly what its name suggests; used for modifying light.

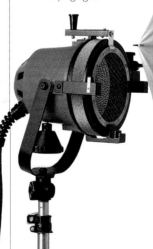

Umbrellas may be used as reflectors (light shining into the umbrella) or diffusers (light shining through the umbrella). The cheapest way of creating a large, soft light source.

Windowlight

Apart from the obvious meaning of light through a window, or of light shone through a diffuser to look as if it is coming through a window, this is another name for a soft box.

Tungsten spot with shoot-through umbrella (Photon Beard)

N I G H T   S H O T S

▼

NIGHT IS A POWERFUL CONTEXT FOR CREATING A MOOD. THE NIGHT SKY IS AN UNDERSTANDABLY POPULAR SUBJECT FOR FINE ART WORK AND IS ALSO, OF COURSE, OF SCIENTIFIC INTEREST. THE NATURAL FEATURES OF THE NIGHT SKY CAN BE SPECTACULAR VISUALLY AS WELL AS INFORMATIVE FROM A RESEARCH POINT OF VIEW: WEATHER PHOTOGRAPHY (LIGHTNING AND STORMS, FOR EXAMPLE) AND ASTROPHOTOGRAPHY WOULD FALL INTO THIS CATEGORY.

But these are often very specialist areas. For the majority of commercial photographers, location night shots present a challenge to capture a good sense of mood and visual impact while working with minimal or virtually non-existent natural lighting. Many of the photographers featured in this book choose to work solely with the available light, however little that might be, and others explore the options of using additional lighting. One alternative is to light the location scene just enough to bring out the detail of the setting, raising the ambient level only to record the scene without losing or altering the atmosphere; another is to re-create the illusion of night in the studio. Whether working for an advertising or editorial client, or creating fine art work, or producing experimental work, the night photographer has a multitude of practical considerations to take into account. It is important, above all, to have a good understanding of how very low light levels work, taking into consideration relative contrast levels and how different film stocks react, especially when dealing with reciprocity failure, in order either to get the best out of the available light or to create a convincing night-time look in the studio.

CAMERAS, LENSES AND FILMS FOR NIGHT SHOTS

During dusk and early morning, at the extremes of the night period (late evening and early morning), it is obviously important to be able to work quickly and with a lot of flexibility because light changes very quickly at these times of day. Roll film cameras and 35mm cameras are therefore probably the most appropriate choice, although it is equally possible to work swiftly with a good field 4×5 camera, as long as you are well prepared with plenty of sheets of film loaded beforehand.

However, once darkness has fallen and night has well and truly set in, it is unlikely that there will be quick, dramatic changes of lighting, and this allows an easier pace of working – unless of course you are photographing lightning, which is both quick and dramatic! When photographing subjects such as lightning and fireworks it may be useful to use a heavier camera on a strong tripod with cable release to give maximum stability for what might be long or short exposures at short notice.

Ideally, the lenses in the photographer's kit will have fast maximum relative apertures as this will help with low lighting levels. Of course, it is not always desirable to shoot with the lens wide open as this makes focusing

very critical, especially with longer lenses, but it is good to have the option of a very large aperture. However, these lenses are vastly more expensive as they are very costly items to manufacture.

Night photography is one genre where some practitioners choose to use negative film over slide film because it has far more latitude, and because colour balances can be altered in the printing stage at the laboratory. Transparency film has a latitude of about one stop whereas with modern negative materials the photographer might reasonably expect a latitude more in the region of 7–10 stops – a very useful practical advantage. Nevertheless, some photographers still prefer to work on transparency film. More often than not, such factors as what stock the photographer favours at the time and any preferred method of working will come into the equation.

LIGHTING EQUIPMENT FOR NIGHT SHOTS

For location night shots, the photographer's technique has to encompass working with the lack of light that is intrinsic to this genre. Many of the shots in this book use only the available ambient light, often at very low levels, and for such work no additional lighting equipment is needed. When additional lighting *is* required, portability will be a major consideration. Location shoots may require the use of battery powered heads, portable generators, or even lorry-mounted generators, if lots of power is required and there is no local supply conveniently available to be tapped into. The usual array of bounces and reflectors may occasionally also be useful.

The studio shoot will require authentic-looking rendition of night lighting by artificial means. For this, it is important to know exactly what the aim is: should the set-up emulate sunset, deep night, moonlight…? The choice of equipment following on from this decision is fairly simple and obvious. A standard head with a lens can take the place of the moon, positioned at an appropriate angle; pin-prick lights, gobos or computer controlled variable lights can be used for stars; and a well-painted backdrop in conjunction with appropriate coloured gels over a focusing spot can be very convincing for a dusk or dawn sky look.

LOCATION OR STUDIO?

The choice of whether the shoot is to take place on location or in the studio will be determined by the purpose of the photograph. In many cases, an advertising or editorial image is needed with a night-time setting as a background for a product or lifestyle image, to create a certain ambience. A studio shoot may be more appropriate for creating exactly the right details and "look" that the client has in mind. The studio session also has the convenient advantage of allowing the shoot to take place during the day as well as all night! This is a factor which may be important to the client in terms

of availability of personnel to attend.

The location shoot is the only option when a picture of a genuine night scene is required, whether the night sky is the main subject or not. It is worth remembering that computer technology can enable you to change day-time shots into night-style images by using appropriate digital filters. But for the "real thing", there is no alternative but to be in the right place at the right time, and the logistics of organising this can be considerable.

LOGISTICS OF THE LOCATION NIGHT SHOOT

Location photography, whether during the day or night, brings with it a host of practical considerations. Sensitivity is always required and it is important to think ahead and anticipate any possible problems. If, for example, the photographer is planning to photograph a location such as a motorway, it is a good idea to inform the local police beforehand of the intention to do so to avoid any undue alarm. It is helpful to supply a full written brief, to register where and when the shoot will be taking place. A wise precaution is to be sure to take an official contact name and number to have to hand in case of any challenge. Similarly, photographing potentially sensitive buildings may require the same kind of preparation and possibly even permission. Another consideration is whether the subject of the shoot is private property, and whether an image of it, even if taken from a vantage point on public property, can be used commercially. Permission needs to be sought and obtained before time and

money is invested in the session. It is a good idea to keep documentation of clearance to hand during a night shoot since any challenge is likely to come from security night staff who may not be aware of any such agreement, and the person who authorised the shoot may well not be available to clarify the situation outside normal office hours.

Safety during a location shoot at night is of paramount importance, as it is likely the photographer will be working in a dark place, not easily seen, and may be preoccupied and not always aware of possible danger approaching. If there is any possible risk from passing traffic or other third parties, it is sensible to alert any relevant bodies of your plans beforehand, and to wear fluorescent clothing at the location. Remote and lonely locations may also bring other worries and it is important to leave with a responsible person full details of where the shoot is being held and what the schedule is, in case of accident. A mobile telephone is of course invaluable, especially as many night shoots are undertaken by a lone photographer with no colleague on hand in case of difficulty. Finally – don't forget to take a torch!

THE LOCATION NIGHT PHOTOGRAPHER

As already mentioned, the location photographer often works alone, in many cases simply because of the unsociability of the time of the shoot. One good aspect of this for many photographers is the element of autonomy in working alone. On the other hand, responsibility falls solely on the photographer's shoulders so, to avoid wasted time and effort, it is essential to get a clear brief agreed with the client beforehand.

Practical arrangements, too, will fall on the photographer's shoulders when there is no assistant present: there is no substitute for being well prepared personally. It is wise to visit the intended location during daylight to recce the possibilities for the shoot, and to assess any practical difficulties or dangers that may not be apparent in the dark. Several subsequent visits will familiarise the photographer with the location, and additional preparatory visits at the appropriate time of night will give an invaluable "cold run" at navigating the area in darkness.

THE STUDIO SHOOT

The team for a studio shoot will often consist of the photographer, an assistant, possibly a model, stylist, hair and make-up artist and an art director. Representatives of the client may wish to be present too. Good studio practice is important for coordinating the various interested parties, making sure everyone is in the right place at the right time, and it is always helpful if everyone is well briefed before the shoot starts so that all know exactly what their role is and what is expected of them during the session.

The fact that the shoot is aiming at a night effect does not hugely alter good studio working practice, except inasmuch as those present should be aware that, with such low light levels, care needs to be taken physically in the potentially dimly-lit studio, as safety is always an important consideration. It may be worth pointing out that if representatives of the client need light to view story boards,

hold discussions or read material during the shoot, there may not be enough ambient light in the studio for their requirements. If this is the case, space should be made available elsewhere, where the lights can be turned on without disturbing the shoot. Another possibility is that the photographer can set up a video "tap" and send the viewfinder image to a monitor in a separate room so that clients can view progress on-screen, whilst carrying on with their own discussions and work in adequate office surroundings. This has the double advantage of providing for clients' needs while also avoiding unnecessary disturbance of the photographer at work.

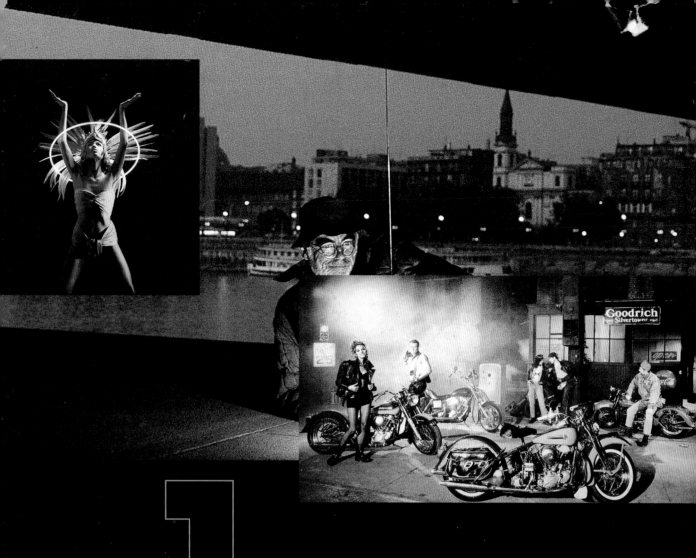

1
night life

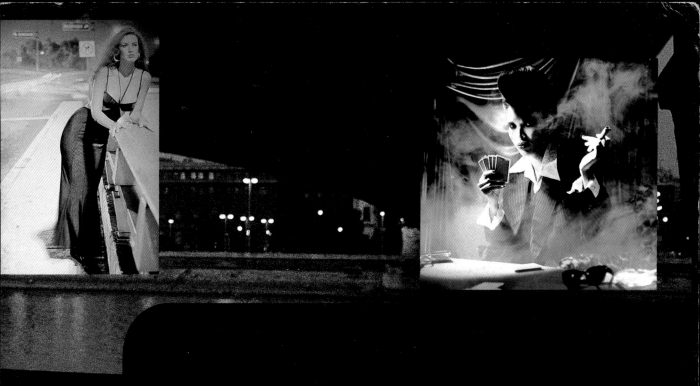

When one thinks of night life one also thinks of night-clubs, discotheques and city street life. These images bring to mind a range of atmospheres and moods, borne out by the range of shots in this chapter. While some of these are portfolio personal work, others are product and advertising shots that play on the glamour (or lack of it) associated with the night world. The moods created range from the underworld of gangsters and dossers to teen street culture and sophisticated night-clubs.

Common to them all is a sense of excitement and, almost inevitably, a "city" feel – night life, it seems, is an urban phenomenon; at least for the photographer. For this reason, many of the images tend to be location city street shots or else interiors of night-associated settings such as night-clubs, which for practical purposes are often set up in the studio rather than on location. Only one shot (Günther Uttendorfer's "Harley Davidson", pages 24-25) is a studio session on a set that is carefully constructed to look like an outdoor location.

Photographer: **Benedict Campbell**

Client: **Personal work**

Use: **Portfolio**

Model: **Danielle Lewis**

Assistant: **Lee Rex Atherton**

Stylist: **Us!**

Camera: **6x6cm**

Lens: **80mm**

Film: **Velevia rated at 150 ISO**

Exposure: **f/8**

Lighting: **Electronic flash**

Props and background: **Yes, lots!**

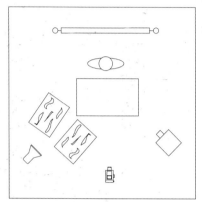

Plan View

▼

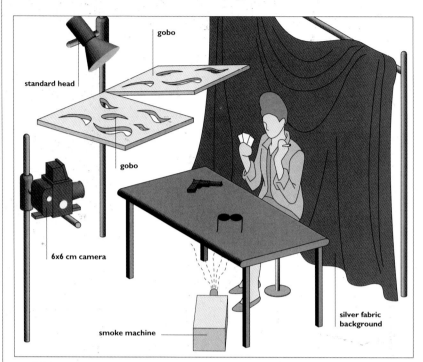

"THE LIGHTING HAD TO PORTRAY A DARK, ALMOST SINISTER, UNDERWORLD FEEL," SAYS BENEDICT CAMPBELL. THE SMOKY ATMOSPHERE WAS LIT BY A STANDARD HEAD WITH REFLECTOR, HIGH UP AND POINTING STRAIGHT DOWN, CAPTURING THE SWIRLING TEXTURE OF THE CLOUDS OF SMOKE BUT STILL ALLOWING SOME VISIBILITY OF THE SUBJECT BEHIND THE SMOKE. TWO GOBOS WERE POSITIONED TO SEPARATE THE LIGHT INTO DISTINCT SHAFTS TO CREATE THE ATMOSPHERIC, MOODY POOLS OF LIGHT IN THE FINAL IMAGE.

The same light, positioned as it is to one side of and high above the model, gives top/side lighting on the face and hands leaving the other sides of the arms and hair in areas of deep shade (again, mottled from the gobo shading).

The silver fabric background picks up the light in interesting ripples and the careful use of props gives contrasting areas of high and low lights in very close juxtaposition, making use of the effect of the gobos; notice the dazzling ashtray and pitch-black sunglasses right next to each other. The blueness of the image was introduced at the printing stage.

► *Lighting smoke from different angles gives totally different effects*

► *The position of gobos in relation to the light source and subject determines the degree of "focus" of the shafts of light. Gobos close to the light source give an indistinct mottling effect while gobos positioned relatively close to the subject give more distinct separate shafts of light*

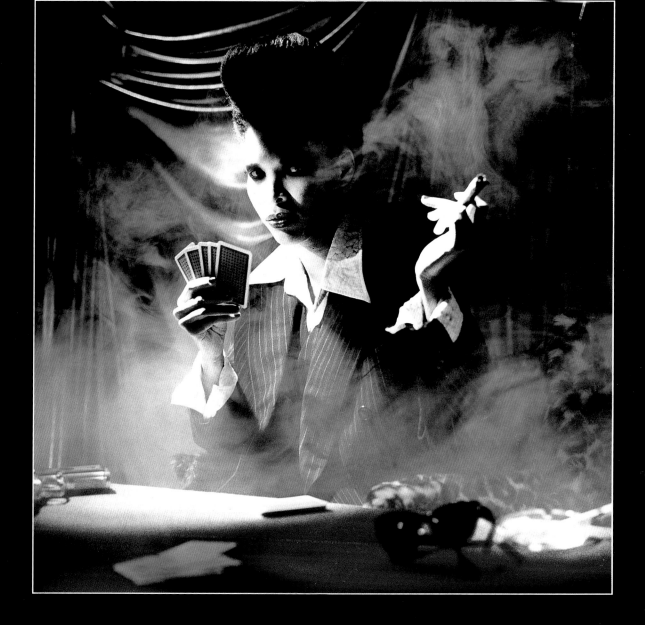

Photographer: **Lewis Lang**

Use: **Exhibition/Print sales**

Camera: **35mm**

Lens: **35mm**

Film: **Kodachrome 64**

Exposure: **1/8 second at f/2.8**

Lighting: **Available light**

Props and background: **Bus stop, Fort Lee, New Jersey**

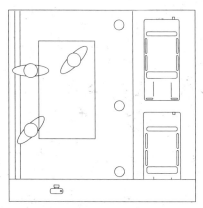

Plan View

► *Bracketing your exposure in 1/3 or 1/2 stops can give you extra "insurance" shots in contrasty night-time situations, where the correct exposure may not always be the best exposure*

► *A spot meter or a camera with spot metering facility is a very useful tool for the night photographer*

THE LONG NIGHT AHEAD

▼

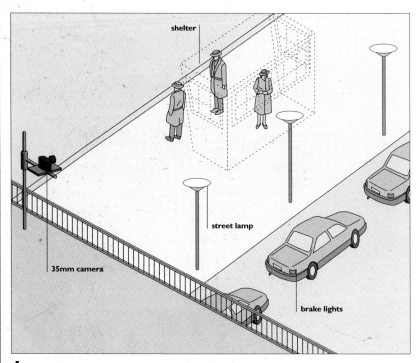

INTERESTINGLY, LEWIS LANG TOOK THIS HAND-HELD SHOT FROM THE SAME OVERPASS WHERE HE TOOK "RUSH HOUR (DETAIL)" ON PAGES 140-141, BUT FOR THIS SHOT HE WAS POINTING THE CAMERA IN THE OPPOSITE DIRECTION.

With such large expanses of dark there is a risk of over-exposing if you don't meter from the correct area of the scene. In this case Lewis Lang took a spot meter reading from the woman in red to make sure that the central and most important part of the image was correctly exposed, despite the dark surrounding area.

He also makes the most of the composition that presented itself, capitalising on the theatrical overtones of the setting. The people waiting look like actors illuminated on a stage; this seems to be a bleak moment in some particularly gloomy play. Our vantage point is the view of a member of the audience seated high up in a box or balcony, remote and removed from the centre stage, out in the blackness. The scattered city lights add the impression of pin-pricks from theatrical lights suspended above the action: the exposure time of 1/8 second at f/2.8 records the car lights as sharp spots, rather than as trails, to add to the illusion.

Photographer's comment:

Vene, vidi, vici (rough translation: "I came, I saw, I photographed").

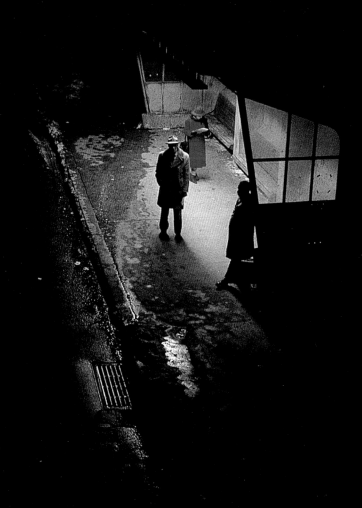

Photographers: **Ben Lagunas and Alex Kuri**

Client: *Vogue*

Use: **Editorial**

Model: **Sandy Posseti**

Assistants: **Natasha, Victoria and Suzanne**

Art director: **Nôe Aqudo**

Stylist: **Felix**

Camera: **Hasselblad 205TCC**

Lens: **180 cf Sonnar**

Film: **Kodak EPP**

Exposure: **3.5 seconds at f/8**

Lighting: **Available light**

Location: **Street**

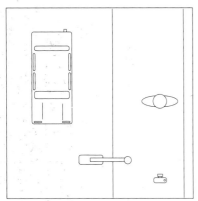

Plan View

N I G H T   F A S H I O N   I

▼

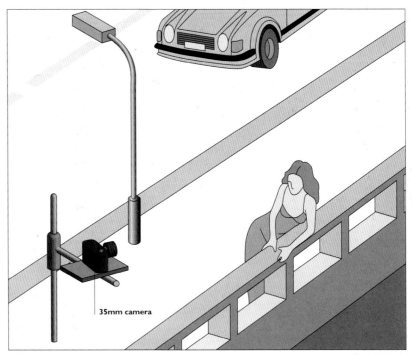

35mm camera

Compare this shot with Night Fashion II (page 129) to see what a huge difference can be achieved in mood and effect, even thought Ben Lagunas and Alex Kuri were using the same model in a similar pose in each shot, in two similar street settings, with similar available street light.

► *The use of a daylight balanced film with street lighting (which could easily be either tungsten, sodium or neon) produces very warm flesh tones and the orange background colour*

► *It can be interesting to experiment with different combinations of film balance and light source. Although this is recognisably a picture of a night scene, it is not night as we see it but a surreally coloured version of night as the chemicals record it*

There are two things that determine the shutter speed – which in this instance is far more important than the aperture (because depth of field is not the priority in this shot). First, the exposure time needs to be long enough for a passing car to drive through the shot. Second, it is obviously important that flesh tones should be correctly exposed. For a model to hold a pose, 3.5 seconds is a long time but it is interesting to note here that although there is no noticeable movement in the body, there is a slight softness to the hem of the dress, perhaps caught by a gentle breeze or air turbulence caused by the passing car.

Photographer's comment:

The lines in the background were produced by the cars passing by.

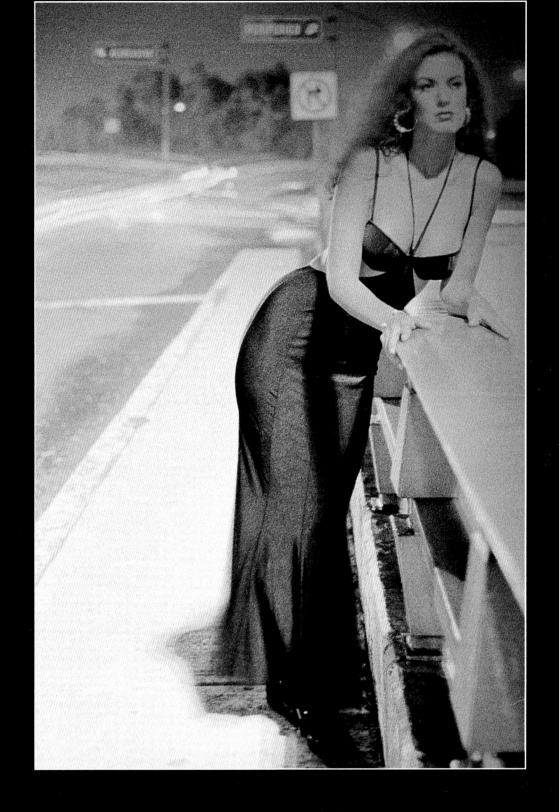

HARLEY DAVIDSON

Photographer: **Günther Uttendorfer**

Client: **Harley Davidson**

Use: **Poster**

Models: **Sonya, Carlos, Renata, Michael, Florian**

Assistant: **Jurgen Weber**

Art director: **Dieter Lopskarn**

Camera: **35mm**

Lens: **50mm**

Film: **Polapan**

Exposure: **f/11**

Lighting: **Tungsten, flash**

Props and background: **Factory inside location, all visible props set up, fog machine.**

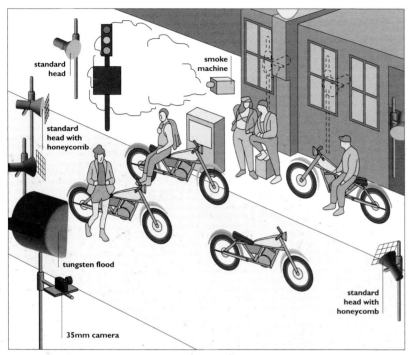

O PPOSING SHADOWS ARE NOT A CONCERN FOR A NIGHT-TIME STREET SCENE AS THEY WOULD BE FOR AN EMULATED SUNNY DAY SHOT: IT IS THE NATURE OF A CITY STREET AT NIGHT THAT LIGHT FROM MANY SOURCES WILL CAST SHADOWS IN DIFFERENT DIRECTIONS.

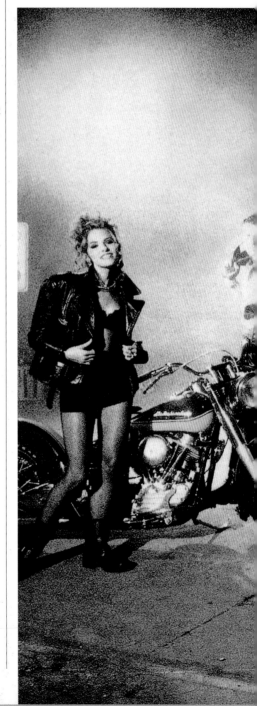

The flexibility and freedom that this kind of scenario gives to the photographer is extremely liberating and introduces the opportunity for exercising a great deal of creative licence. Since this is an advertising shot it is important for the Harleys to be clearly picked out and so as the diagram shows, there is a separate light for each bike and grouping.

The fog machine is positioned out of sight behind the corner of the cafe; you can see some puffs of fog coming out near the Coca-Cola sign. The sign itself is lit by a standard head from behind, pointing in the direction of the camera, to make the most of the cloudy effect of hazy mist. The main groupings in the set each have their own standard head with honeycomb, but the key light is a large flood to the left side of the camera and raised up 3.5m high (as the length of shadow behind the blue Harley indicates).

The cafe interior is lit from within by a flash at each window, in imitation of typical cafe lighting; the ambient glow has been added later by hand.

Photographer's comment:

We had to make an indoor location look like an outdoor location so we shot at night. We needed all day for set-dressing and lighting. Shot in black and white, then hand-coloured.

► *Polaroid Polapan film gives a dramatic Hollywood filmset feel*

► *Fog and smoke are best lit from behind*

► *There are different kinds of "smoke" machines: for example, dry ice (carbon dioxide) and cracked mineral oil, which gives excellent visual results. However, it is important to check what kind of*

vapour will be produced since some vapours can form a coating on the camera lens that is difficult to clean off. The ensuing cleaning process may even scratch and cause permanent damage. An optical flat or a skylight filter (one that is cheap enough to be disposable) should side-step the problem if you are in any doubt

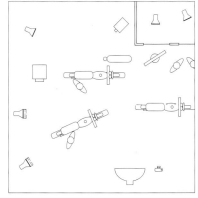

Plan View

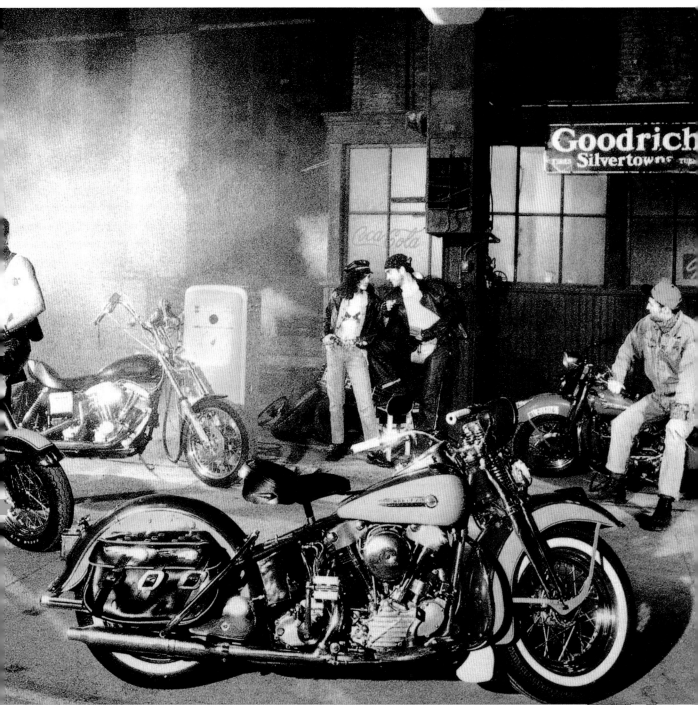

AN OLD DOSSER AND A NEW TRANSISTOR TV

Photographer: **Mike Károly**

Client: **Videoton Co.**

Use: **Panorama poster**

Model: **Gyula Schmidt**

Assistant: **József Jámbor**

Art director: **Mike Károly**

Stylist: **Veronika Chmelár**

Camera: **6x7cm**

Lens: **50mm**

Film: **Kodak Ektachrome 120**

Exposure: **5 seconds at f/5.6**

Lighting: **Battery spot and mini-flash with slave**

Location: **Elisabeth bridge, River Danube, Budapest**

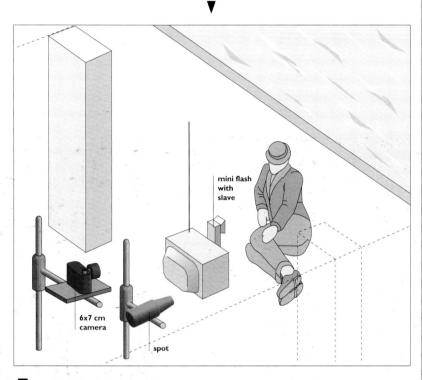

mini flash with slave

6x7 cm camera

spot

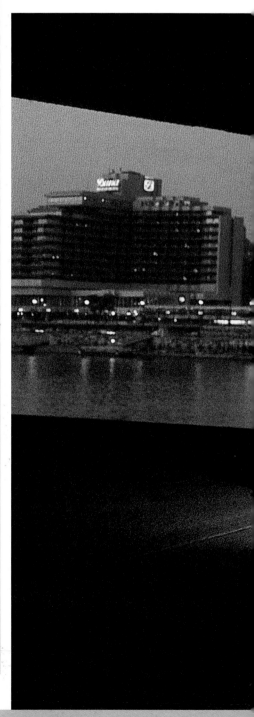

THE MAIN FLASH IS A BATTERY SPOT TO THE CAMERA RIGHT, LIGHTING JUST THE FACE OF THE SUBJECT. A MINI-FLASH WITH A SLAVE-CELL IS TRIGGERED IN RESPONSE TO THE MAIN FLASH, AND IS HIDDEN BEHIND THE TELEVISION, CREATING THE ILLUSION OF LIGHT EMANATING FROM THE TELEVISION SCREEN AND ILLUMINATING SOME OF THE DOSSER'S CLOTHING.

These two sources are carefully controlled to light only the model – and to avoid illuminating the surrounding area of the underside of the bridge.

The shot was taken in early evening, at a time when there was still enough light in the sky reflected in the river to give a blue sweep of water, which provides a degree of separation between the subject and the background. The time of day also means that city lights are on giving interesting reflections and diffraction in the water.

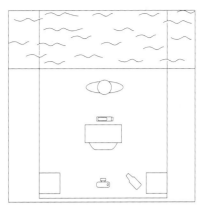

Plan View

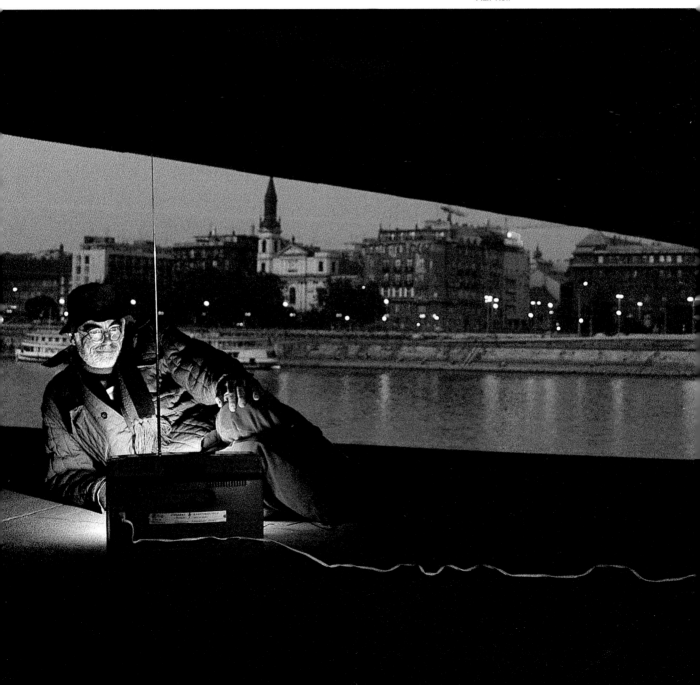

Photographer: **Paco Macias**

Use: **Self-promotion**

Model: **Aurora Robles**

Assistants: **José Luìs Hernandez and**
Gabriela Hernandez

Camera: **6x6cm**

Lens: **150mm**

Film: **Fuji RHP 400 (rated at 800 ISO)**

Exposure: **Double exposure: flash**
followed by neon

Lighting: **Flash and neon**

Props and background: **Neon ring hanging**
from the ceiling

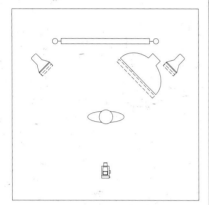

Plan View

► *When inexact lighting or other elements*
are involved, the best way to get exactly
what you want is to bracket
comprehensively; always remembering
to make a note of the settings and
results for future reference

C O P I L L I

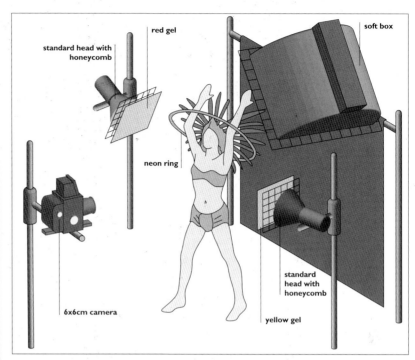

Paco Macias explains that a "copilli" is a feather tuft used by the Aztecs. The picture looks like the result of a long and complicated process, but is actually a fairly straightforward double exposure and was achieved with less fuss than might be imagined. As always, the best approach is "one step at a time".

In the first exposure the model was lit by three heads. Two of these were placed slightly behind the model, one on each side, and both were modified with a honeycomb and a coloured gel. The resulting red tone on the left and yellow on the right is clearly visible in the final image. These lights were aimed at the body and arms with a little of the colour falling on the head-dress too, but this was lit mainly by the larger soft light reflector

positioned further back still which also "keys" the side of the model's face (camera right).

For the second exposure, the model stayed in position in order to block the view of the hoop behind her, but Paco Macias had to find an exposure time that was just long enough for the lit neon hoop to record on the shot without recording a second image of the model.

Photographer's comment:

The mystical pose and wardrobe used by the model, reminds us of the spiritual culture of the Aztecs. The purple light given out by the neon ring combines with the coloured flash light to produce the effect that I was looking for.

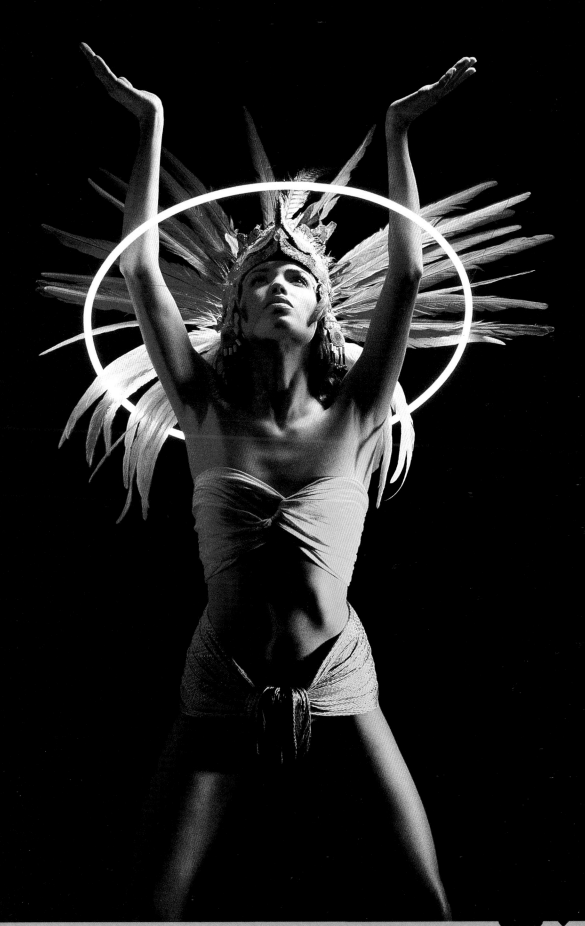

Photographer: **Lewis Lang**

Use: **Exhibitions/print sales**

Camera: **35mm**

Lens: **28mm**

Film: **Kodachrome 64**

Exposure: **1/15 second at f/2.8**

Lighting: **Tungsten street lamp, available light**

Props and background: **a bridge in Grants Pass, Oregon**

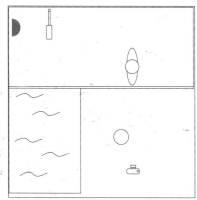

Plan View

THE NIGHT BRIDGE

▼

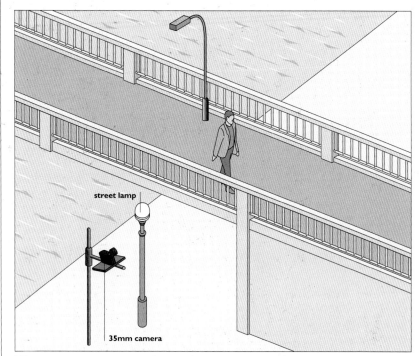

street lamp

35mm camera

THE MAIN LIGHT IN THIS PICTURE IS NOT SO MUCH A SOURCE OF ILLUMINATION AS A SUBJECT IN ITSELF. THE BACKGROUND SKY STILL SHOWS TRACES OF SUNSET LIGHT, ENOUGH TO SHOW THE BRIDGE STRUCTURE IN SILHOUETTE. THE MOON, ALTHOUGH FULL, DOES NOT CONTRIBUTE ANY SIGNIFICANT AMOUNT OF LIGHT; ITS FUNCTION HERE IS TO GIVE SOME DETAIL AND INTEREST IN THE SKY.

Lewis Lang's commentary on this picture provides a useful insight into how one professional approaches the task of composing and taking a strong and saleable image. "I went up close to the lamp and locked on a meter reading, hoping there would be enough glow in the sky to make the bridge stand out in silhouette. Both vertical and horizontal compositions were tried out putting the orange street lamp, bridge, etc., in different parts of the frame. A 28mm wide-angle lens and a steady hand helped me to eliminate camera shake and include the elements I wanted, in the perspective I wanted. The bridge, moon and lamp were good and graphic elements but something was missing. I recognised what that something was when I saw the man walk across the bridge and complete the composition."

► *A light tripod can greatly enhance the sharpness of pictures*

► *If a tripod is not available, using a wider lens may help you to get away with hand-holding*

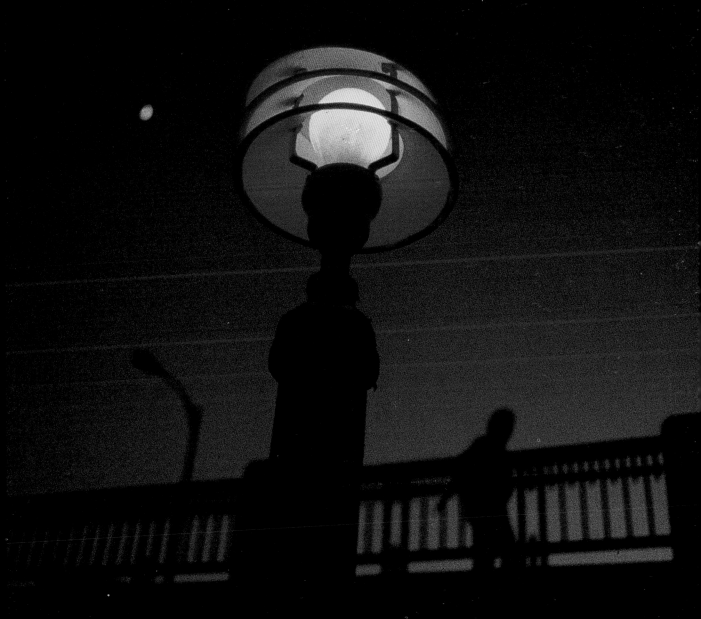

Photographer: **Wolfgang Freithof**

Client: *La Sara*

Use: **Advertising**

Model: **Elena**

Assistant: **Le Gia Quach**

Art director: **Boyd Babbit**

Make-up: **Nikki Wang**

Stylist: **Sophia Lee**

Camera: **35mm**

Lens: **85mm**

Film: **Fuji 100**

Exposure: **4 seconds at f/4**

Lighting: **Electronic flash**

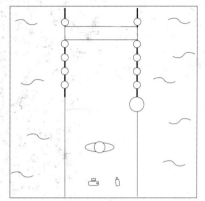

Plan View

GIRL ON BROOKLYN BRIDGE

▼

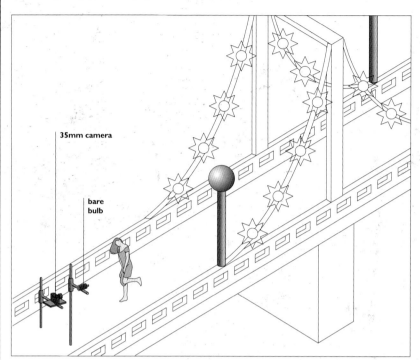

35mm camera

bare bulb

WOLFGANG FREITHOF WAS CONCERNED THAT A LARGE LIGHTING SET-UP WITH WIRES AND CABLES WOULD HAVE CAUSED AN OBSTRUCTION FOR PEDESTRIANS ON THE BROOKLYN BRIDGE, STILL VERY BUSY AT 10 O'CLOCK AT NIGHT WHEN THIS SHOT WAS TAKEN. SO HE MODIFIED AN AUTOMATIC GARAGE DOOR-OPENING UNIT TO ACT AS A REMOTE CONTROL TO TRIGGER THE LIGHT — THUS AVOIDING THE NEED FOR CABLE SYNC LEADS.

The light source itself was a battery-operated Norman 400B bare bulb, chosen for its flexibility and transportability and to provide what the photographer describes as "edgy light". The photographer bracketed at around a 4-second exposure for the ambient lights to record, also allowing the dancing model in shimmering clothing to record with an exciting sense of movement.

The shiny surface of the pavement provides some nice reflections of the floodlights on the bridge structure in the background.

► *Shiny surfaces can give a good sheen of reflected light*

► *Polaroid stock can be invaluable for determining exposure for ambient lighting*

Photographer's comment:

The client supplied me with clothing and wanted a free interpretation from me. Since I was working on a series of night-time shots, the assignment gave me freedom to experiment.

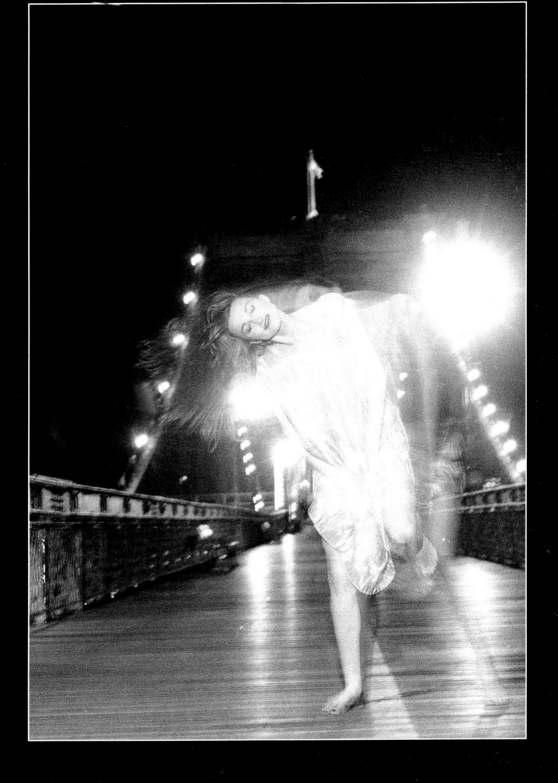

Photographer: **Salvio Parisi**

Client: **Sharra Pagano Necklaces**

Use: **Editorial**

Models: **Eda and Diana**

Assistant: **Chicca Fusco**

Hair and make-up: **Francesco Riva**

Stylist: **Grazia Catalani**

Camera: **4x5 inch**

Lens: **180mm**

Film: **Kodak Ektachrome 64**

Exposure: **6.5 seconds at f/5.6**$^{1/2}$

Lighting: **Electronic flash, 2 heads**

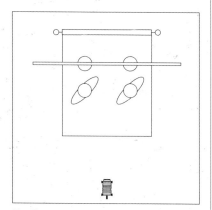

Plan View

► *If you don't have professional snoots to hand, improvise! (But be careful not to create a fire hazard by placing paper too close to a hot modelling light!)*

► *Top lighting can sometimes be unflattering but here it adds to the dramatic effect*

EDA AND DIANA

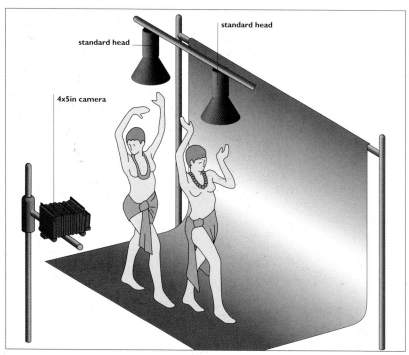

NIGHT-CLUB CONDITIONS OR DEAD-OF-NIGHT CARNIVAL STREET SCENES RARELY OFFER AN EASY TASK FOR A PHOTOGRAPHER; IT IS EASIER BY FAR TO SET UP A SIMULATION IN A STUDIO ENVIRONMENT.

For this shot, Salvio Parisi created a jet-black background with the models emerging into a glare of light. The pose, costume and sense of dancing movement all contribute to an energetic, exuberant mood to set off the flamboyant jewellery that is the *raison d'être* of the shot.

The only lights are the flash heads positioned 2m above the models.

These are modified with two black paper cones directed onto the bodies of the models themselves. The cones snoot the light to keep it directional, and the choice of black paper ensures no bouncing of light so that the models seem to emerge from the deep of the night.

Photographer's comment:

The combination of a direct light from above, the pose of the black models, the deep, dark atmosphere and background give an idea of elegance and mystery but also wildness and strength.

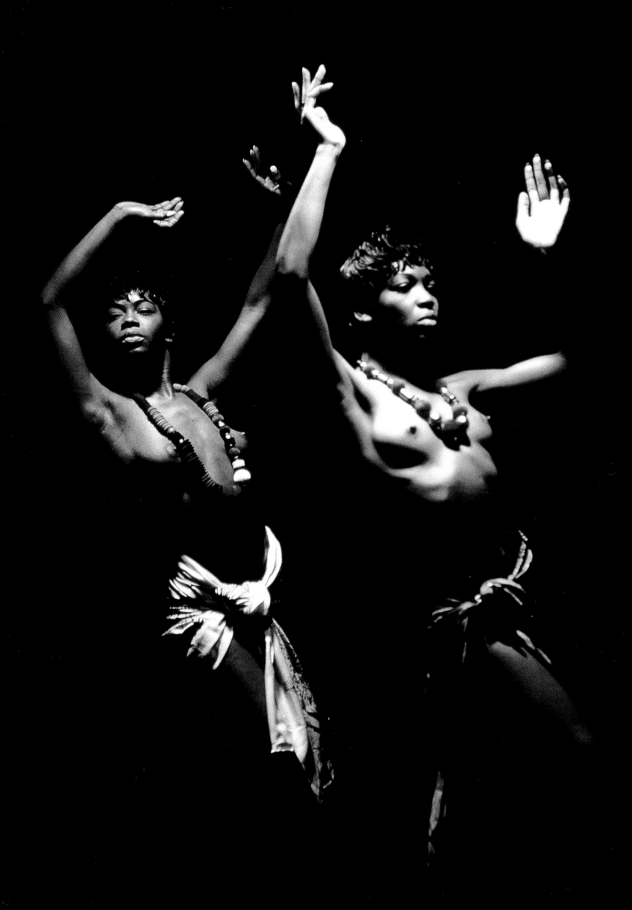

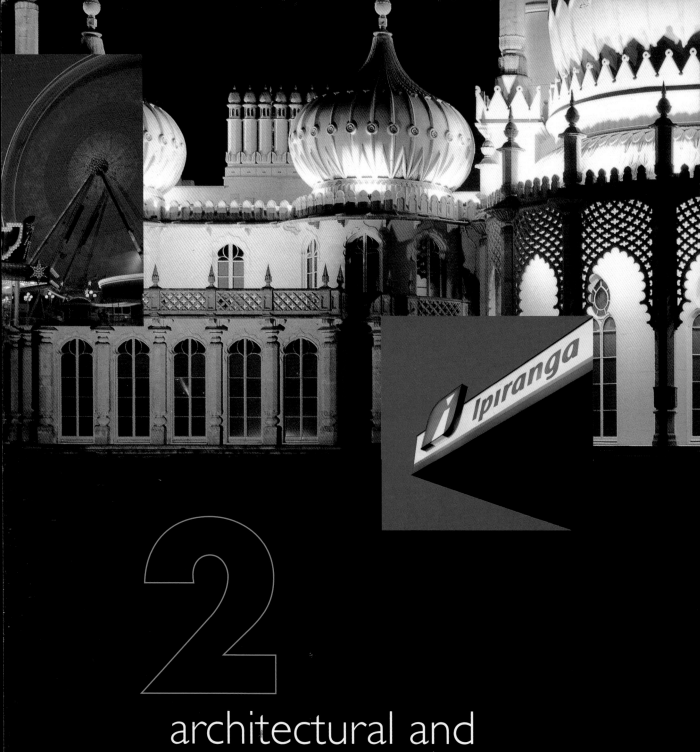

2

architectural and
industrial

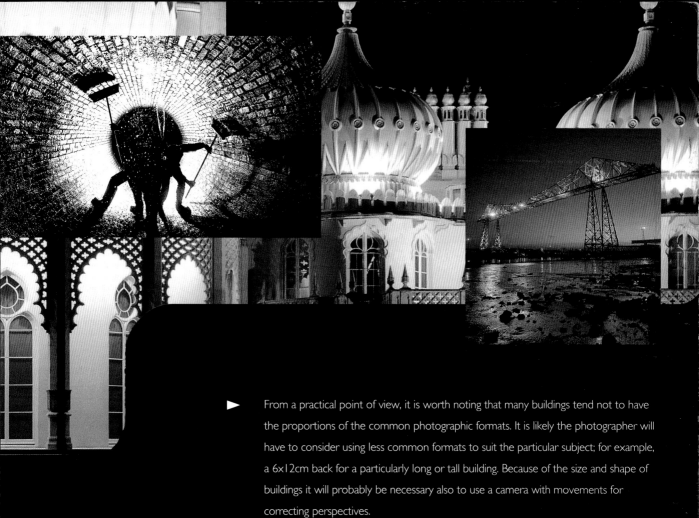

From a practical point of view, it is worth noting that many buildings tend not to have the proportions of the common photographic formats. It is likely the photographer will have to consider using less common formats to suit the particular subject; for example, a 6x12cm back for a particularly long or tall building. Because of the size and shape of buildings it will probably be necessary also to use a camera with movements for correcting perspectives.

Another consideration is that buildings contain people; and a day-time office hours shot of a building is likely to be full of workers, passers-by and the general public, which may or may not be what is wanted. For a person-free portrait of a building, a night shot is an obvious choice. The building can be lit using the night almost as a studio, in that the darkness gives the photographer more control over what lighting will go where than is possible during hours of daylight. The darkness of the night setting also allows the colour and form of even the dullest grey, plain building to be made to stand out against its background, with no undue competition from neighbouring colourful features or overwhelmingly bright blue skies, or the sun itself, of course.

Industrial and architectural subjects are a source of fascination for many photographers because of the inherent variety of designs, textures, forms, masses and unexpected juxtapositions that can occur; a visual treat in themselves. The documentary potential of industrial and working history is also important for some practitioners and can be a powerful source of inspiration.

Photographer: **Mike Károly**

Client: **Self-promotion**

Use: **Calendar**

Camera: **4x5 inch with 6x12cm roll film holder**

Lens: **135mm**

Film: **Fuji Velvia**

Exposure: **8 seconds at f/16**

Lighting: **Available light**

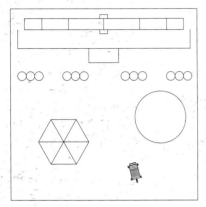

Plan View

B I G   W H E E L

▼

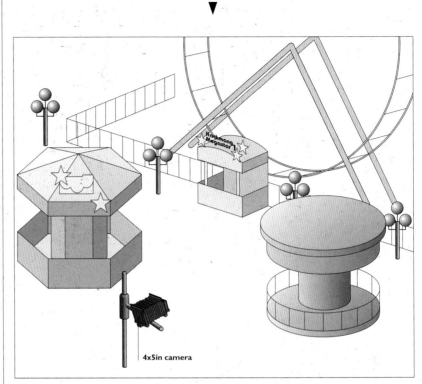

4x5in camera

ALTHOUGH 6x12CM ("PANORAMA") BACKS ARE USUALLY ASSOCIATED WITH WIDE SWEEPING LANDSCAPES, IT IS ALWAYS WORTH KEEPING THEM IN MIND FOR TALL SUBJECTS OR UNUSUALLY PROPORTIONED PORTRAIT-ORIENTED IMAGES.

Here, a fairground big wheel soars above the foreground in an upright "panorama" that successfully conveys both the dizzying height and sheer speed of the ride, yet avoids the problems of perspective distortion of a more typical straight-up-and-down shot. The 8-second long exposure captures the sense of movement while the star-like centrepiece of the wheel and nearby fairground stalls remain sharp and static by contrast. The low colour temperature light bulbs on the fairground stalls and rides in the scene would give a feeling of coolness if photographed with tungsten-balanced film. Instead, Mike Károly chose daylight film to add warmth and atmosphere to the shot, more in keeping with the exhilarating mood of a fairground.

► *With a tall, straight-sided building as the subject, a similar shot might have suffered from perspective distortion, but this can always be corrected (or exaggerated, if required) by using camera movements on the 4x5 monorail camera (that is, rising front).*

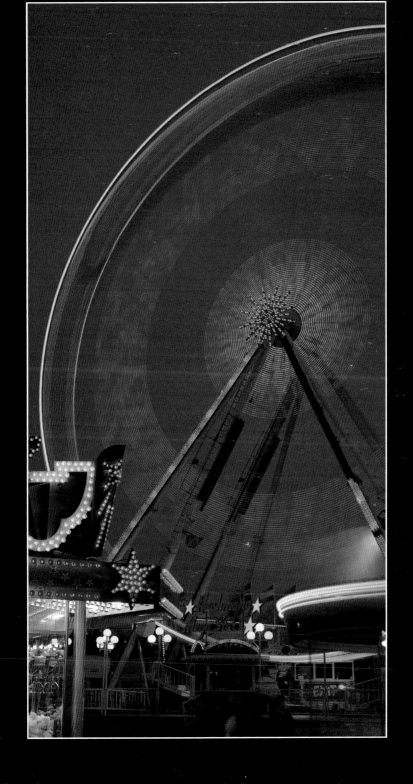

Photographer: **Guido Paternò Castello**

Client: **Ipiranga**

Use: **Calendar**

Assistant: **André Luís Moreado**

Art director: **Frederico Gelli**

Design: **Tatil Design**

Camera: **6x6cm**

Lens: **127mm**

Film: **EPP 100 pushed 1 stop**

Exposure: **4 seconds at f/16**

Lighting: **Available light**

Plan View

▼

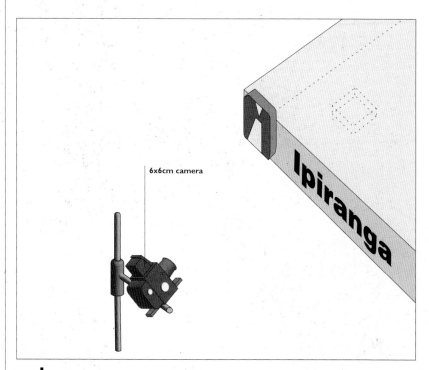

6x6cm camera

IT IS NOT OBVIOUS AT FIRST GLANCE, BUT THIS IS IN FACT A PHOTOGRAPH OF A GAS STATION. OR RATHER, A PHOTOGRAPH OF A DETAIL OF AN ARCHITECTURAL CANOPY OVER A GAS STATION.

► *With some auto-focusing cameras, linear polarising filters can interfere with the focus-sensing mechanisms or give an incorrect exposure reading. Check your manual, or use a circular polarising filter to be on the safe side*

► *When using a circular polarising filter, it is possible to lose up to 3 stops, depending on the orientation of the filter. A longer exposure will be required to allow for this*

► *A polarising filter can also be used as a neutral density (ND) filter*

The form and design of the canopy itself are already strong and graphic, but Guido Paternò Castello has found a composition that maximises the impact of these qualities to the full. To further enhance the graphic potential, he has used a polarising filter on the lens, which has the effect of smoothing and deepening the colour of the already dark evening sky. The canopy sign itself is lit from within and this dictates the exposure. Any unwanted details recorded on the underside of the canopy (for example, textures lit by the small square white light that is visible) were not a worry since digital touching-up was available to eliminate superfluous parts of the image at the next stage. Guido Paternò Castello explains that "the image was digitally manipulated to clean up defects on the structure and the sky."

Photographer's comment:

This image was manipulated digitally on a Power Mac 8100/80 with Photoshop 3.0.

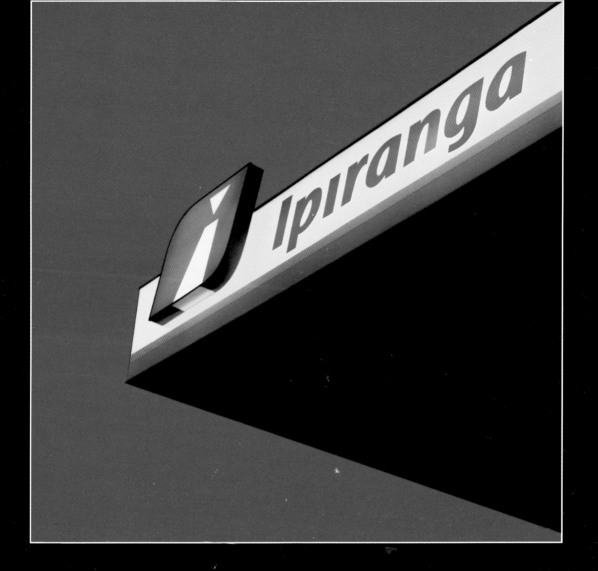

SOUTHERN WATER CLEANING BRIGHTON SEWER

Photographer: **Stewart Goldstein**

Client: **Southern Water**

Use: **Editorial**

Assistant: **Paul Sharkey**

Art director: **Joan Sisley**

Other: **Geoff Loader**

Camera: **35mm**

Lens: **20mm**

Film: **HP5 Plus**

Exposure: **1/60 second at f/8**

Lighting: **Electronic flash**

▼

torch

torch

lumedyne flash

35mm camera

Prize-winning work may be of the most unlikely subject matter. This stunning award-winning shot by Stewart Goldstein was a commission from a water company for a photograph of workers making a final cleaning check before the opening of a sewer.

The graphic form of the tunnel is in itself something of a dream subject, with the wealth of textures and forms in the bricks and structure, and the hypnotic perspective of the walls leading to who-knows-what in the deep black circle beyond.

The legs of the three workers are silhouetted against the gleaming illuminated areas of the wall while their upper bodies merge with the gloom of the passageway extending away from the camera, with just a trace of rim light defining their outline, giving a surreal, science-fiction feeling that is heightened by the star-like droplets of water spraying through the air. The tunnel wall is back-lit by an assistant some distance down the tunnel holding a lumedyne, and a small amount of fill on the near side is provided by two torches which are just enough to reveal the texture of the bricks closer to the camera.

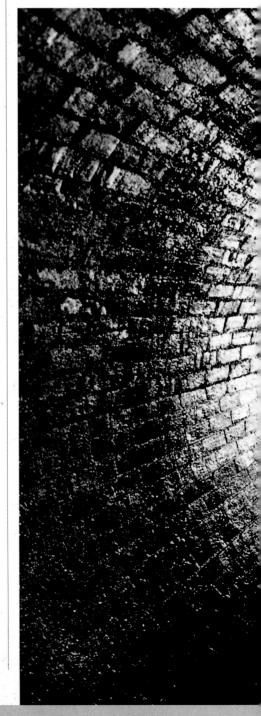

► An exciting graphic form in a subject can be a great inspiration but needs to be lit appropriately to realise the potential

► Reflective wet surfaces give fascinating shadows and reflections. Notice the curvature of the shadow of the broom on the right in contrast to the straightness of the handle itself

► Guinness Award for Best Black and White Picture. Selected for exhibition in the Royal Photographic Society/Kodak International Exhibition of Prints

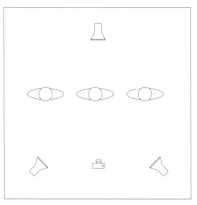

Plan View

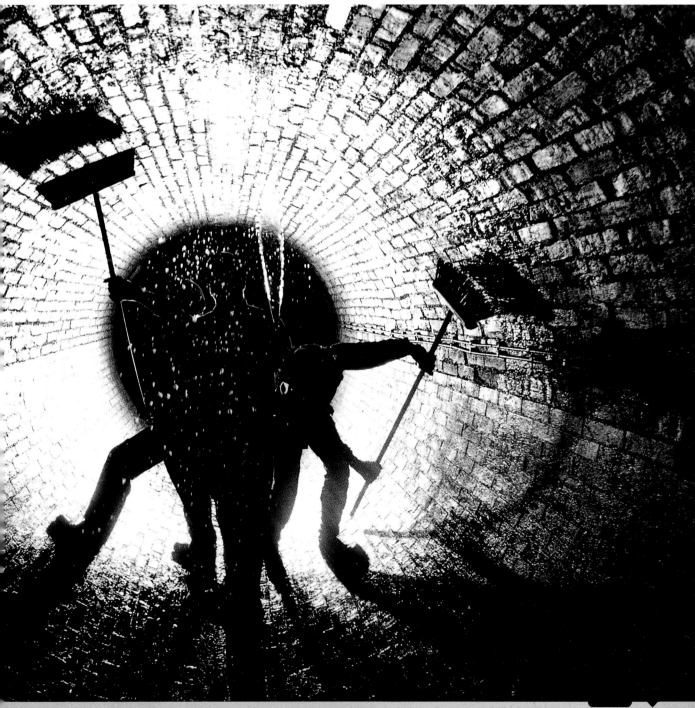

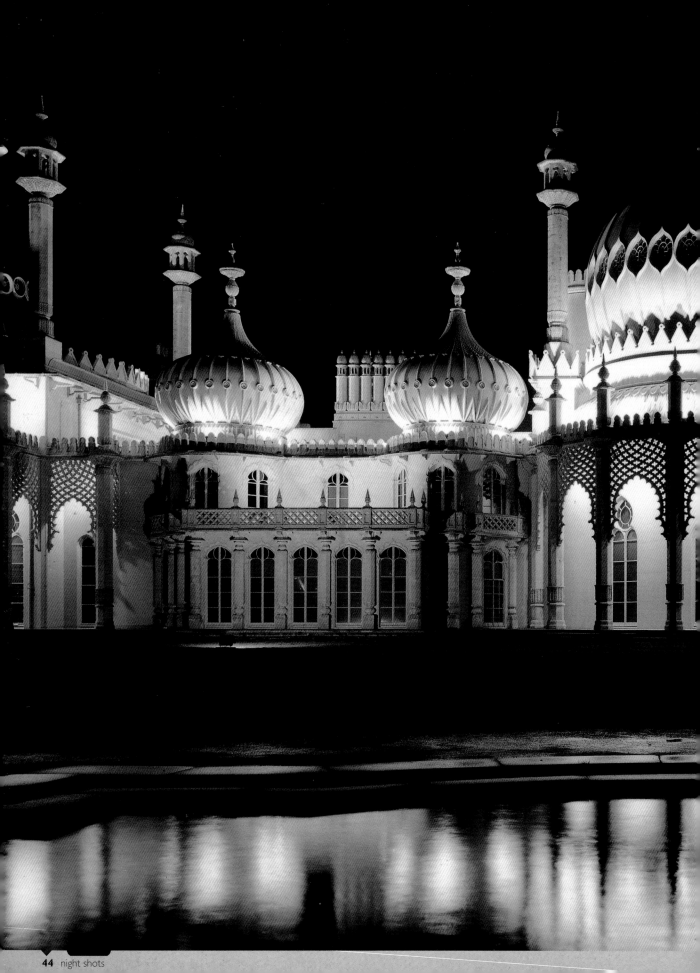

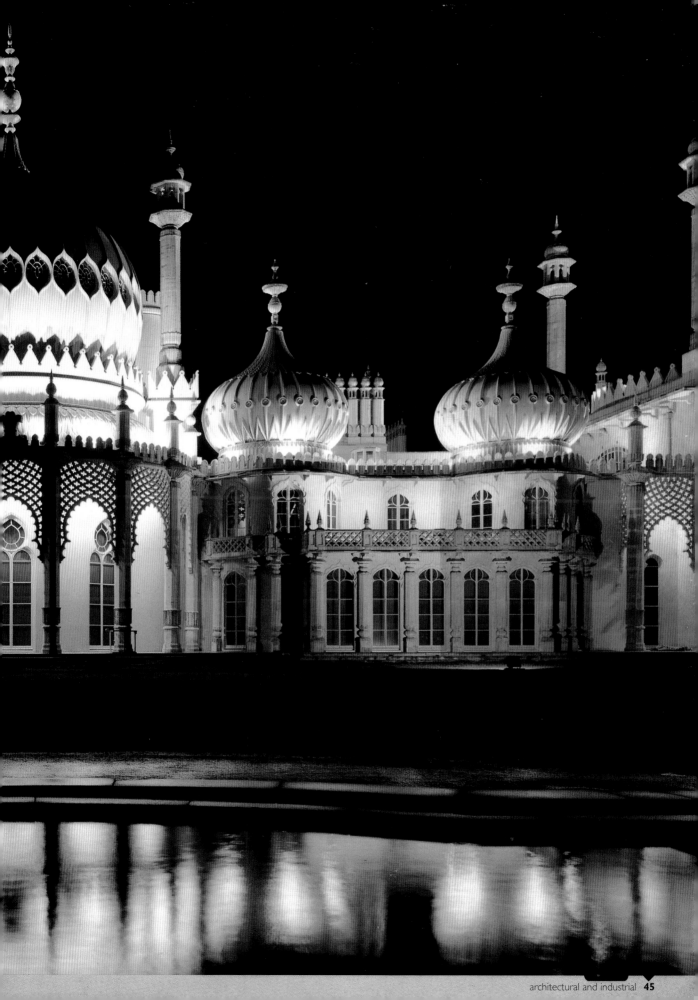

Photographer: **Tim Hawkins**

Client: **Philips**

Use: **Promotional**

Camera: **4x5 inch**

Lens: **90mm Super Angulon**

Film: **Kodak VHC 100**

Exposure: **1 second at f/22**

Lighting: **Available lights on building**

Props and background: **Brighton Pavilion**

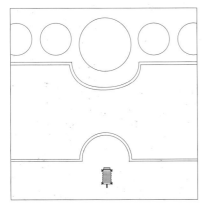

Plan View

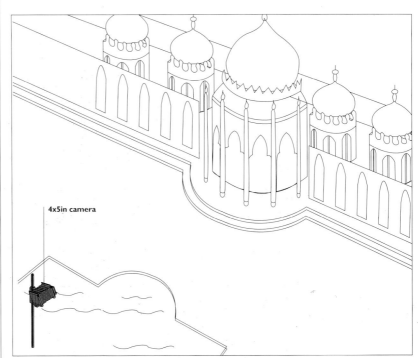

"THE PROBLEM IS CREATING SOMETHING IN THE FOREGROUND WHEN IT IS JET BLACK," SAYS PHOTOGRAPHER TIM HAWKINS. "THE SURROUNDING AREA WAS MESSY BUT I FOUND THE POND AND USED IT FOR REFLECTION TO GIVE BALANCE AND ADD INTEREST."

The camera was about 12 inches above the water with a good viewpoint of the reflection. At the same time Tim used a lot of drop front and a small amount of front tilt on the 4x5 camera to correct the perspective.

Only ambient light was used; in this case, the expertly arranged lighting scheme designed by Philips especially to illuminate the Pavilion. This is a tungsten-based source, giving a brown/yellow glow in this shot (because the film used was not a tungsten-balanced stock).

► *Permission may be needed to shoot in the grounds of private property*

► *A thorough recce at different times of day will give good insight into the variety of shots that can be achieved at a location*

Photographer: **Tim Hawkins**

Client: **Philips Lighting**

Use: **Editorial**

Camera: **4x5 inch**

Lens: **65mm**

Film: **Kodak VHC 100**

Exposure: **1/2 second at f/16 1/2**

Lighting: **Available light**

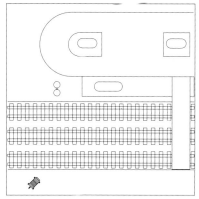

Plan View

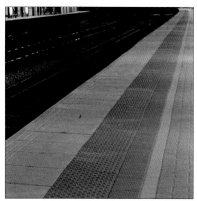

Detail

► *Kodak VHC has been discontinued and replaced by Pro Gold 100 HC*

► *Load films in advance if time is going to be short and there is no assistant available*

► *Polaroid Polapan has a quick processing time, ideal for doing tests in a situation where time is short*

► *A tight crop emphasizes the strong geometric form of the subject*

ASHFORD INTERNATIONAL RAILWAY STATION

▼

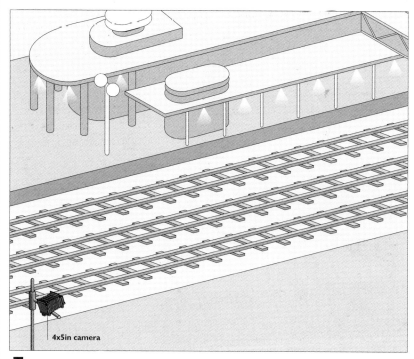

4x5in camera

TO MAKE SURE HE GOT JUST THE RIGHT TWILIGHT SKY FOR THIS DUSK PICTURE, TIM HAWKINS LOADED EIGHT SEPARATE SHEETS, SHOOTING AT ABOUT 7 MINUTE INTERVALS. HE NEEDED THE SKY TO BE DARKER THAN THE STATION LIGHTING, SINCE THE STATION LIGHTING WAS THE WHOLE POINT OF THE SHOT.

The sun was setting to the right of the frame, gradually giving an increasingly rich dark blue in the sky in the area recorded as the upper left corner of the frame here. It wasn't until Tim could see the rich blue colour that he began to shoot, when this part of the sky was one or two stops darker than the station subject. Tests using Polaroid Polapan were done to check the contrast between the building and the sky.

Photographer's comment:

Even though this is Ashford Station in England, officially I was in France when I took this picture because you have to go through passport control to get to this platform!

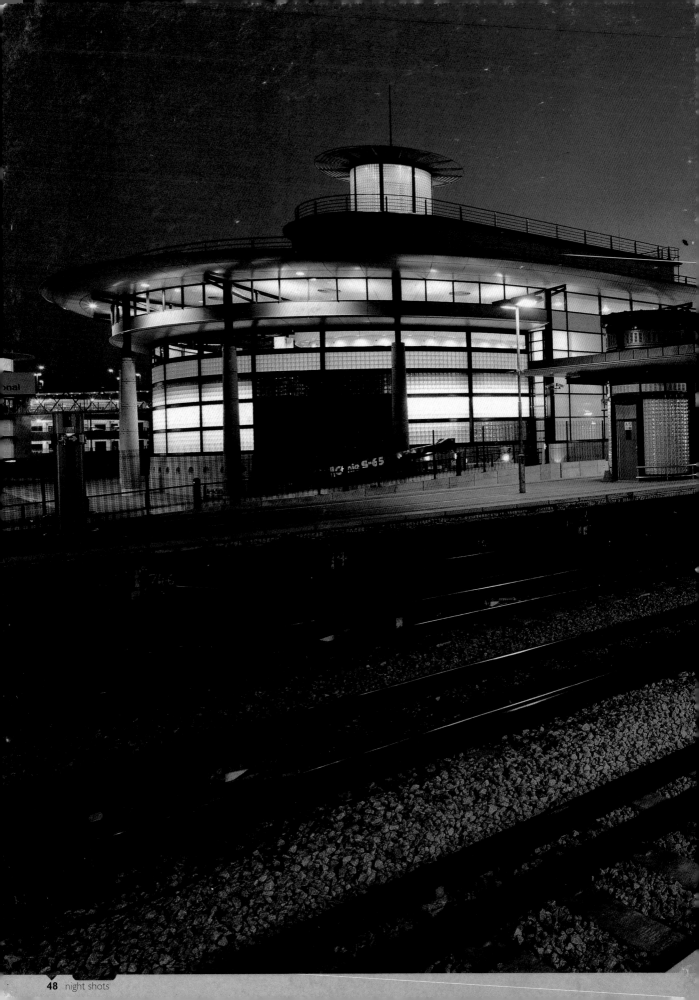

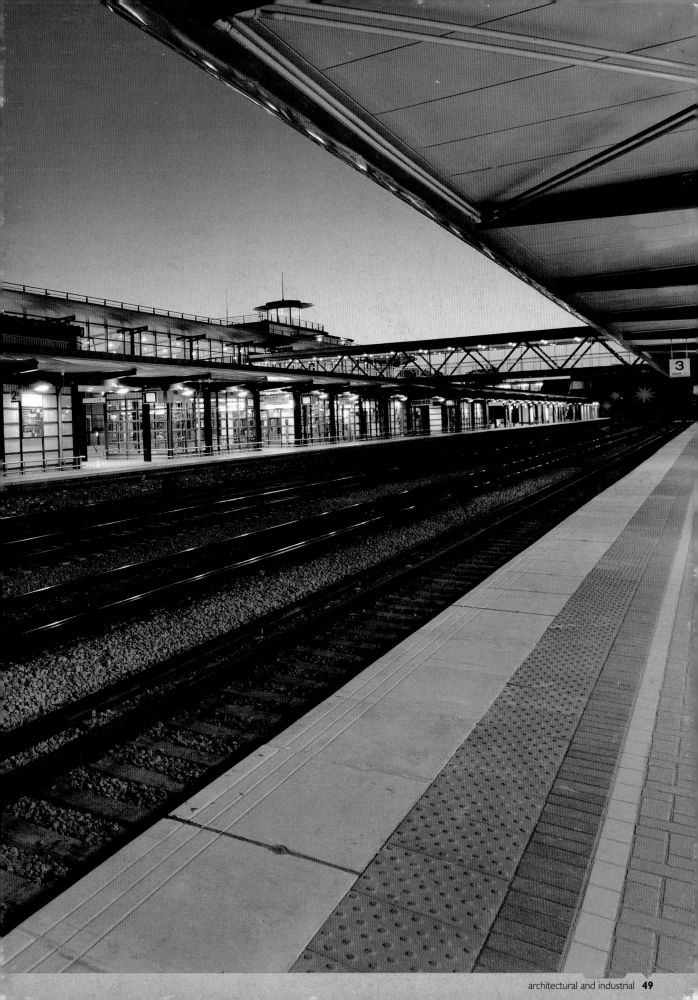

Photographer: **Chris Rout**

Camera: **RZ67 Pro-II**

Lens: **50mm**

Film: **Kodak EPX 64X**

Exposure: **2 minutes at f/11**

Lighting: **Available light**

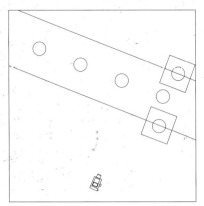

Plan View

▼

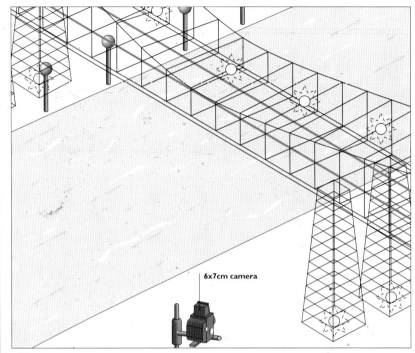

6x7cm camera

Ektachrome 64 is a relatively slow film for this kind of shot, so to capture the colour and texture in the shoreline debris at the bottom of the frame a full 2 minute exposure was needed.

With an exposure of this length, the sky would normally burn out and give a result that was far to bright. To counter this possibility, Chris Rout used a soft-edged graduated pink/mauve filter at the top of the frame. Notice that although the filter adds colour to the upper part of the picture (sky), it is positioned so that it does not distort the colour of white lights on the bridge. It is interesting to see that the predominant colour of the shoreline and nearest water areas of the picture is a deep grey-blue; the position and graduation of the filter have obviously ensured that the additional mauve tone has not been applied to this area of the photograph.

The wider lens combined with a large depth of field (aperture of f/11) helps to achieve the sharpness of the foreground.

► *Restrained use of coloured filters*
can enhance the effect, but beware
lurid and unconvincing results from
over-rich filters

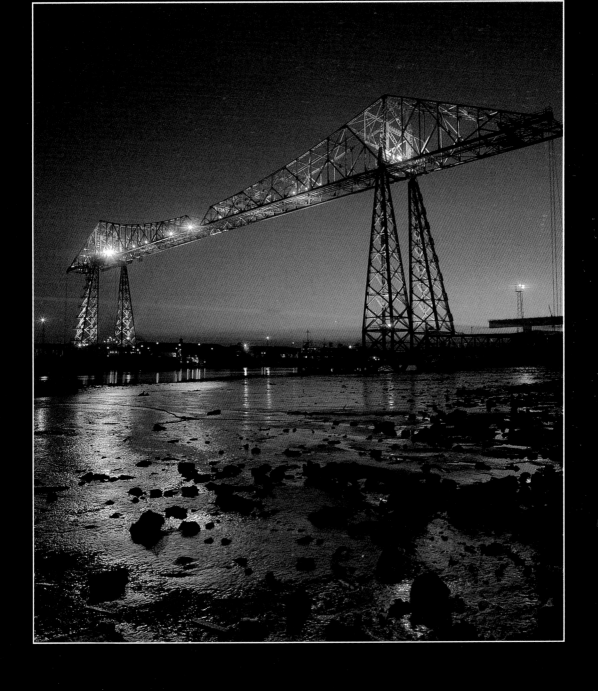

Photographer: **Agelou Ioannis**

Use: **Self-promotion**

Camera: **Mamiya RB67**

Lens: **90mm**

Film: **Fuji Velvia 50 ASA**

Exposure: **10 minutes at f/8**

Lighting: **Multiple on-camera flash**

Props and background: **Camera set on Gitzo Tripod with standard heavy-duty head**

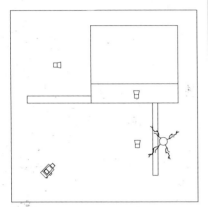

Plan View

▼

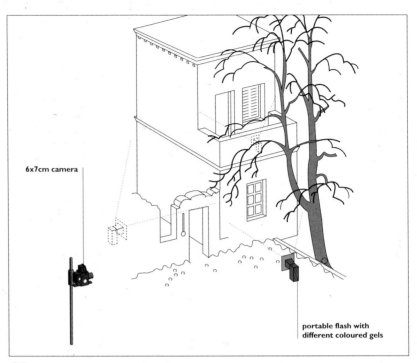

6x7cm camera

portable flash with different coloured gels

MULTIPLE FLASHES WERE FIRED AT SELECTED AREAS OF THE SUBJECT BUILDING TO CREATE THIS INTRIGUING SHOT. THE HAND-HELD PORTABLE FLASHGUN WAS USED WITH COLOURED GELS TO GIVE THE REQUIRED COLOURS ON DIFFERENT AREAS OF THE BUILDING.

Agelou Ioannis explains how the shot came about: "A fellow photographer had spotted the place. The original idea was a promotional image for a colour separation house, but we eventually came up with a still-life for their campaign and we retained this image for our own use.

"A couple of rolls were shot after a Polaroid test was taken. The trick was to create a colourful image without the photographer (dressed in black) or the firing tube being seen in the final picture. The flash must have been fired around twenty or so times for each part of the image."

► *Bear in mind that different gels will have different densities and therefore will vary the output of the flash to different degrees. Tests will need to be done to determine the required metering*

► *It may be necessary to snoot the flash head to avoid spill light and overlapping colours on particular areas of the subject*

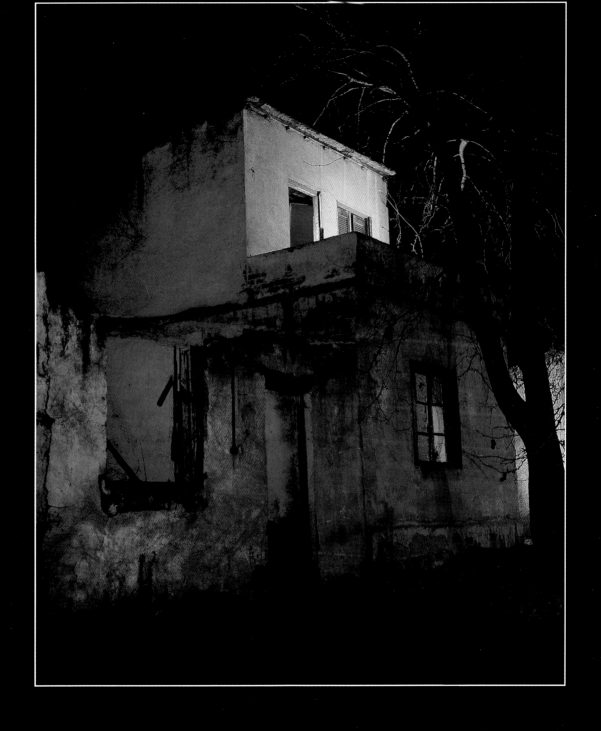

COOLING TOWERS

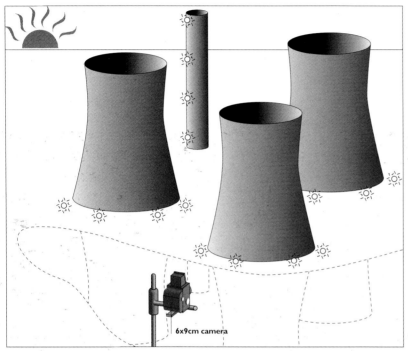

6x9cm camera

Photographer: **Alex Larg**

Use: **Editorial**

Camera: **Mamiya Press**

Lens: **90mm**

Film: **Kodak Ektachrome 400**

Exposure: **8 seconds at f/22**

Lighting: **Available light**

SILHOUETTE CAN HAVE A STRONG IMPACT IF THE SILHOUETTED ITEMS HAVE A POWERFUL FORM. THE BOLD CURVES AND SHEER SOLID MASS OF THESE COOLING TOWERS CONTRAST WELL WITH THE GHOSTLY VAPOUR DRIFTING FROM THEM, WHICH IN TURN MERGES WITH THE CLOUDS, GIVING AN IMPRESSION ALMOST OF A CLOUD FACTORY AT WORK.

Reflection is another powerful visual tool, and the small dots of red light on the straight, slender chimney just left of centre, provide additional interest both above and below the reflection line.

This photograph demonstrates that you don't need absolutely brilliant back light or absolute darkness in the foreground to achieve a stark silhouette effect. The sun here had been below the horizon for about half an hour, so although the background sky still had

colour and light, it was certainly not bright. And since there was ambient early evening light at the site, the near side of the cooling towers were still quite clearly visible. The relative difference of light, rather than the absolute level of light is what is more important. Use of contrasty fast film exaggerated the difference, and ensured that the cooling towers came out as pure silhouette showing none of the detail of structure and texture that was clearly visible to the naked eye.

Photographer's comment:

I really love the shape of these cooling towers. I just have to stop and photograph them every time I go past.

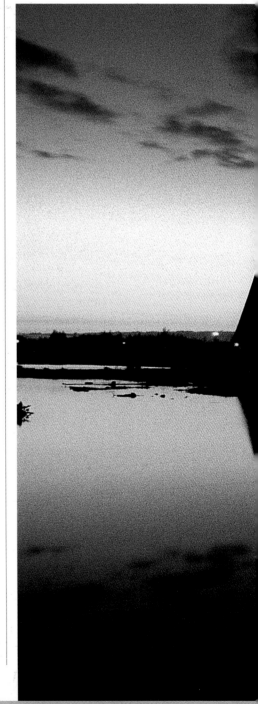

► You can learn a lot about light by studying the same location at different times of year and different times of day

► Experiment with a combination of shutter speeds and apertures to see how clouds of steam or smoke record for comparative lengths of apertures

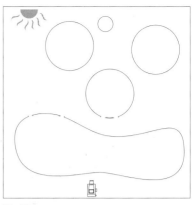

Plan View

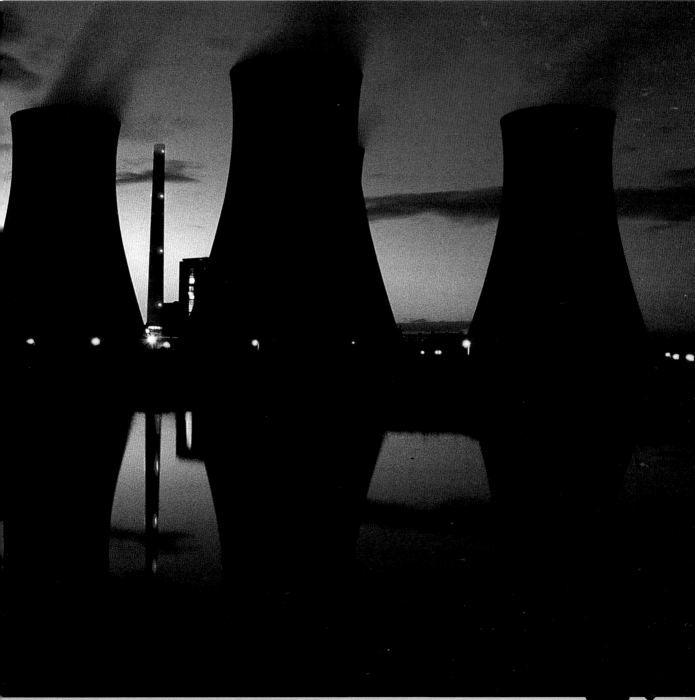

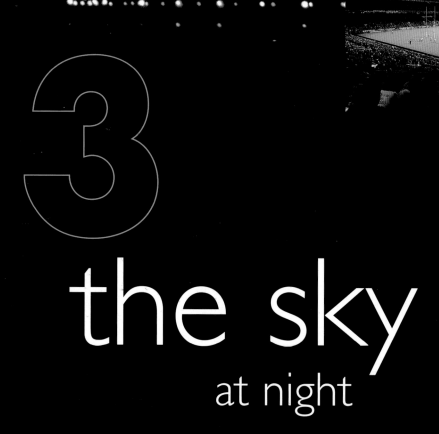

3

the sky
at night

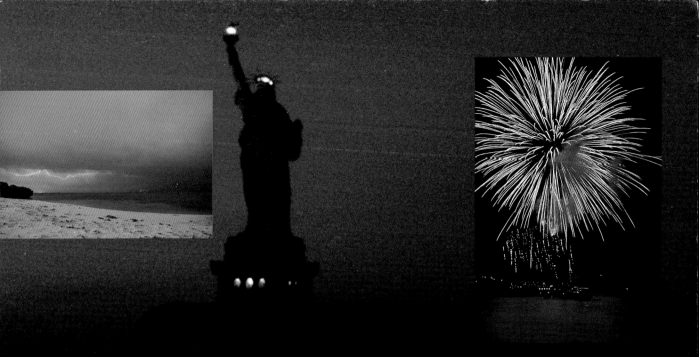

The work featured in this chapter tends to be from the hands of specialists in their field. So many things can be seen in the sky at night – and so many things are beyond the human eye. Many photographers specialise purely in aspects of the night sky and the work of some such practitioners is featured in this chapter. Also included are examples of work where the sky plays a major role in the composition and descriptions of the practical considerations necessary to achieve a particular kind of shot; considerations which often recur with a variety of types of subject matter. Lightning and fireworks, for example, have something in common; the fleeting pyrotechnical display has to be caught swiftly and has to register well against a night sky backdrop.

The astrophotography shots included here are the specialism of Tony and Daphne Hallas, and are all taken with feet (and camera) firmly on the ground of Planet Earth, however space-bound they may appear. The camera and astro-telescope reveal far more than is available to the naked eye.

For most of us, the night sky as it is seen by the naked eye is more than enough of a challenge. How can the photographer record it convincingly? And what if there is competition in the frame from an enormous amount of artificial lighting in the foreground – say, in the form of a sports stadium illumination? The technicalities of striking a balance are again specialist skills.

Photographer: **Bob Coates**

Client: **VI Business Journal**

Use: **Editorial newspaper cover**

Camera: **35mm**

Lens: **35–135mm set at approximately 40mm**

Film: **Fuji Velvia RVP 50**

Exposure: **3.5 seconds**

Lighting: **Available light**

Props and background: **Amalie Charlotte**

Harbour, St Thomas

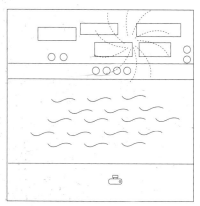

Plan View

FIREWORKS

▼

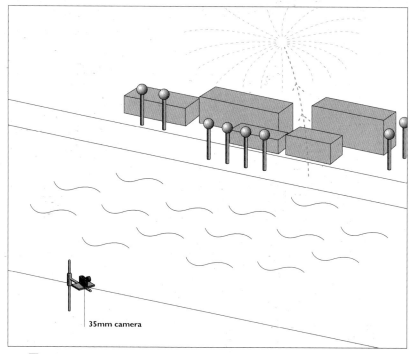

35mm camera

THE BRIGHT RED REFLECTION ON THE WATER OF THE VIRGIN ISLANDS COMES PURELY FROM THE RED OF THE EXPLODING FIREWORKS, NOT FROM ANY FILTRATION OR SPECIAL EFFECTS TREATMENT.

With expert timing and precision, Bob Coates has captured the excitement and glory of a stunning carnival fireworks display, set off by the dramatic setting of Charlotte Amalie Harbour, complete with illuminated ship at centre stage. Of course, for a long exposure of this kind it is essential for other details to be stationary; the boat in swift motion would not have recorded so effectively.

The fireworks were recorded by holding the shutter open for 3.5 seconds, allowing plenty of time for the full explosion of the firework to take place and for the trails to record. Ending the exposure crisply at just the right moment is important, as the falling sparks of the disintegrating explosion would detract from the flower-like form captured here.

► *For long outdoor exposures you must use a very heavy tripod and cable release*

► *If the conditions are windy, put extra weight on the tripod to keep it steady*

Photographer's comment:

Calm nights over water are best. Hold the shutter by feel. Hold the shutter open longer for multiple bursts.

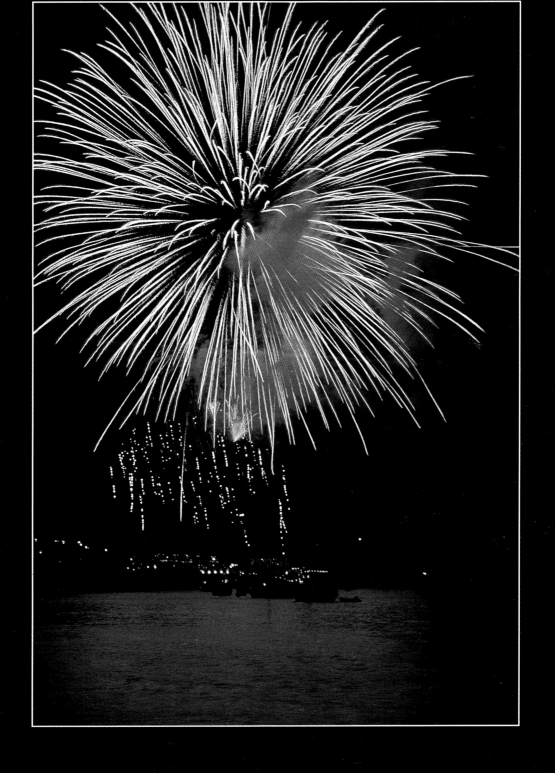

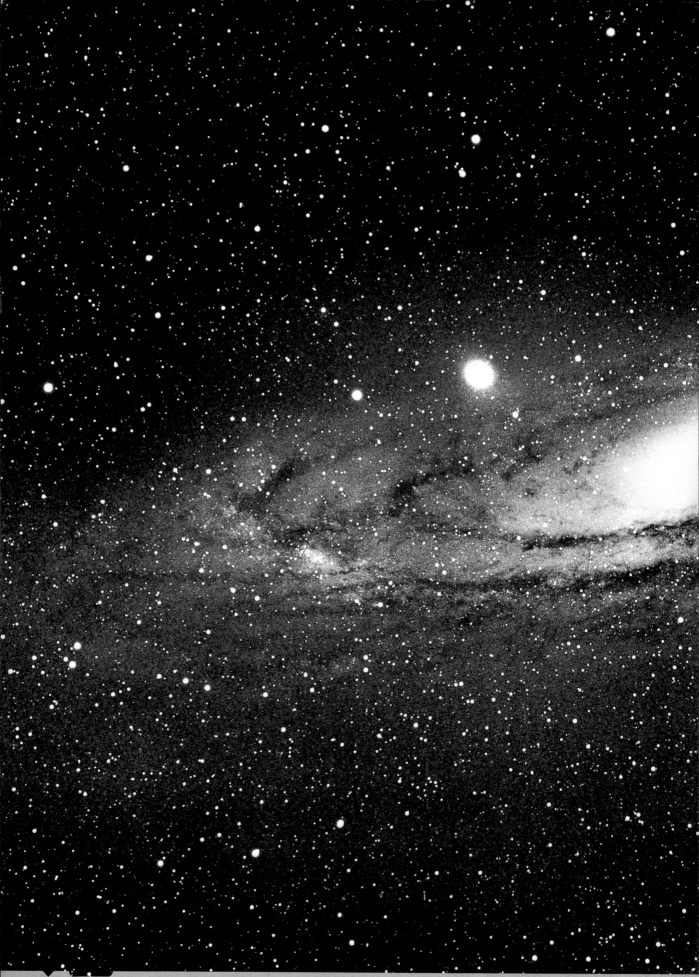

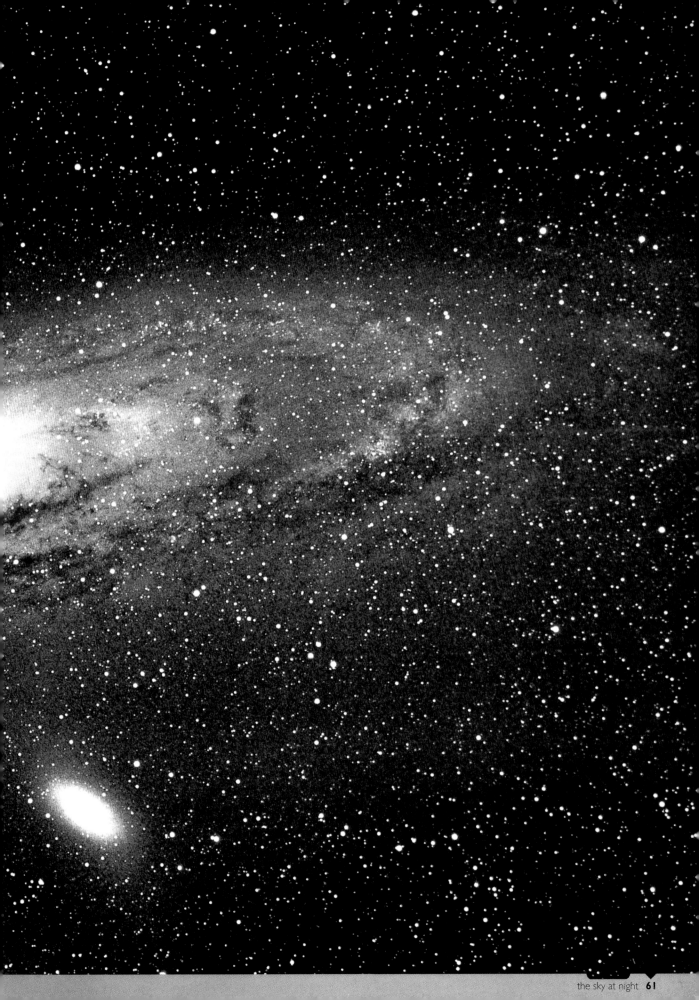

Photographers: **Tony and Daphne Hallas**

Use: **Stock**

Camera: **Pentax 67**

Lens: **6 inch f/7.5 Apo refractor**

Film: **Fuji SHG 400**

Exposure: **50 minutes**

Lighting: **Available light**

Photographers: **Tony and Daphne Hallas**

Use: **Stock**

Camera: **Pentax 67**

Lens: **165mm f/4**

Film: **Fuji SHG 400**

Exposure: **25 minutes at f/5.6**

Lighting: **Available light**

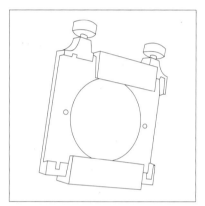

The interface connects the telescope and the camera.

ANDROMEDA GALAXY M31

▼

THE RHO OPHIUCHI NEBULA

▼

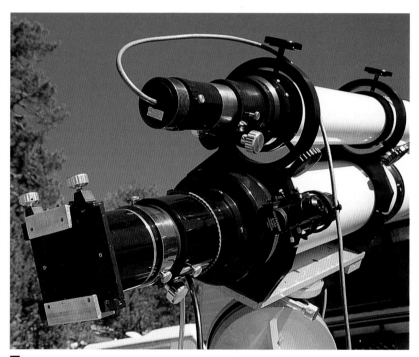

THE HIGHLY SPECIALIST OCCUPATION KNOWN AS ASTROPHOTOGRAPHY IS, UNSURPRISINGLY, AN EXTREMELY DIFFICULT FORM OF PHOTOGRAPHY. NOT ONLY DOES IT REQUIRE A LARGE AMOUNT OF SOPHISTICATED EQUIPMENT (INCLUDING TELESCOPES AS WELL AS CAMERA EQUIPMENT, OF COURSE), BUT IT ALSO DEMANDS CREATIVE, PATIENT AND DEDICATED HUMAN RESOURCES.

► *The camera must be carefully mounted on the telescope to ensure the desired result*

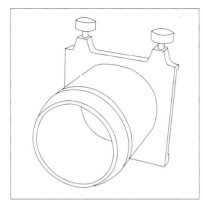

A tube leads to the telescope.

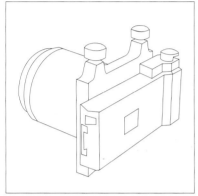

Mounted on the other side of the telescope.

► *The special attachment allows the camera to be mounted in precisely the right position*

Tony and Daphne Hallas of Astrophotography are based in Oakville, California in the USA, though judging by these shots, typical of their work, one could be forgiven for concluding that their studio must be on a new-age space station somewhere Out There.

However, the hallmark of the renowned work of the Hallases is that their astronomical shots are not taken from outer-space stations or craft, but amazingly are achieved from earth, with the aid of powerful telescopes specially designed for the purpose.

Stunning shots of this calibre and subject matter are attempted by very few people in the world and are successfully achieved by even fewer. The Hallas team are renowned throughout the astronomical and astrophotography world for their extraordinary work and are certainly masters in the field. Although it is true to say that the equipment, techniques and opportunity to develop this particular expertise are simply not available to many practitioners, the chance to gain an insight into the secrets of their extremely specialist endeavour is nevertheless truly fascinating, for curious professionals in other fields and other accomplished astrophotographers alike.

The most important specialist tool for astrophotography is, of course, the telescope. The actual choice of telescope can be crucial, and experimentation is in this field, as in so many photographic areas, invaluable.

"We have used many telescopes throughout our photographic years," says Tony Hallas. "These have included a Celestron 14inch mounted on a 12inch Schaefer mount, and 5inch, 6inch and 7inch Astro-Physics refractors. Currently we are using the 7inch f/7 Astro-Physics refractor on the 12inch Schaefer mount."

The choice of camera, by contrast, is a familiar choice for professional photographers of many kinds.

"We are beginning to use a Pentax 6x7 inch camera," says Tony. "This is used with a 165mm f/2.8 lens for the ultra wide field images, fastened to the Astro-Physics 400 mount. For most of our colour work we use hyper-sensitised Fuji 400 film in 120mm format and 35mm."

The two shots featured here, of the Andromeda Galaxy and the Rho Ophiuchi, were taken using much the same technique.

In the case of the Andromeda Galaxy, the initial image was made by exposing two Fuji SHG 400 negatives sequentially with an Astro Physics 6inch f/7.5 Apo refractor. The exposure time for each negative was fifty minutes.

These two negatives were then stacked one on top of the other – obviously taking great care to ensure that the images of the stars were in perfect registration. This "sandwich" of negatives was finally exposed onto 4x5 Vericolor print film positives. During this step, standard dodging and burning was done to bring out the fainter elements of detail.

Two of these VPF transparencies were then combined in registration and contact-printed onto a 4x5 inch internegative film. The exposure was adjusted to yield the desired contrast. This becomes the "master negative" from which all subsequent images are made.

The Rho image was created using basically similar technique, though with some variation in exposure times used, as necessary.

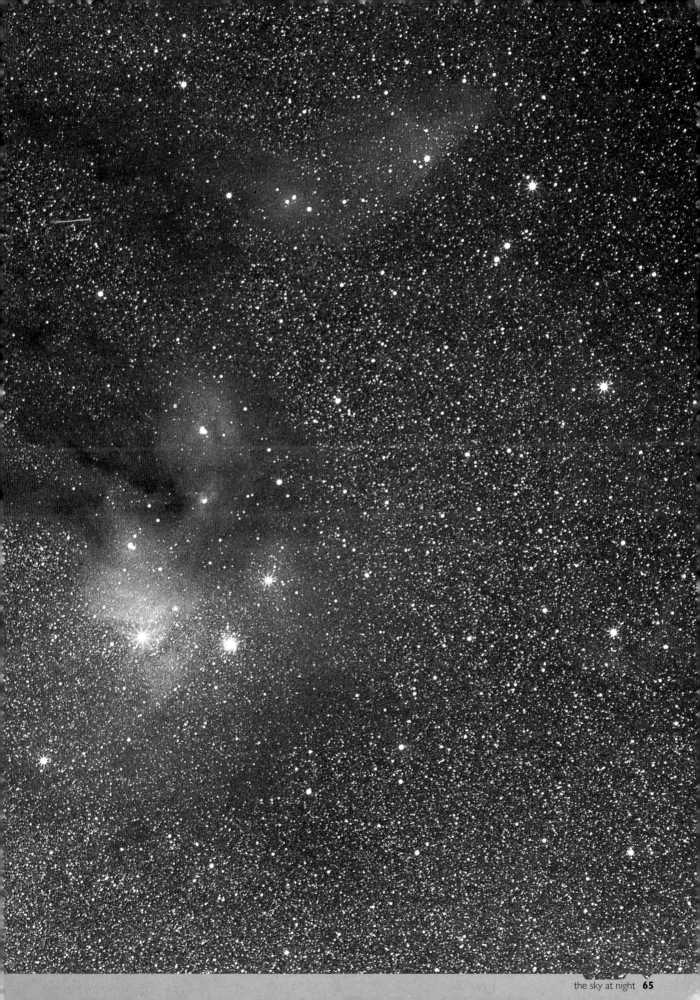

Photographer: **Nick Djordjevic**

Client: **Self-promotion**

Use: **Calendar, fine art prints**

Camera: **Nikon F4**

Lens: **28mm**

Film: **Kodachrome 64**

Exposure: **3½ minutes at f/4**

Lighting: **Available light (lightning)**

Props and background: **Ocean Reef, Perth**

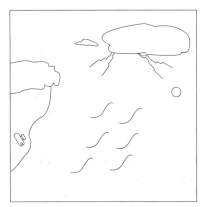

Plan View

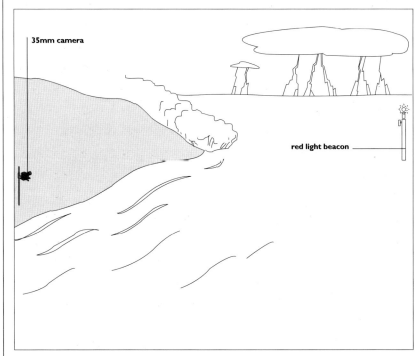

35mm camera

red light beacon

Nick Djordjevic has made a specialisation of the area of the Perth coastline near his home in Australia, and is a maestro of stunning lightning, skyscape and landscape shots, using only ambient light. .

This shot and the two images that follow were all taken from the same vantage point at different times, using various focal length lenses.

At first glance it may seem unlikely that this set of shots with such different moods and ambient light coloration could possibly have been taken all at the same place. But notice the details of the setting which confirm that this is indeed the case: the beacon with red lights, the outline of the rock formations and general lie of the land are all evidence of the fact.

The sequence represents a case in point demonstrating the importance of understanding available lighting conditions and the extent to which such insight allows a hugely versatile range of results. One of the hallmark features of Nick

Photographer's comment:

Available as a fine art lithographic poster.

Djordjevic's distinctive work is that despite appearances, he never uses colour filtration or special processing or printing special effects techniques to add the extraordinary colour tints that are such a strong feature of his work; a fact that many find difficult to believe. The important thing is that all three shots demonstrate how very much ambient light can vary and how differently this records on film under different conditions.

"For the technically minded, one of the biggest surprises about my photography is that I don't use any colour correction, colour balancing, or special effects filters and I don't use flash or coloured gels," says Nick. "Apart from using an ultra-violet, or skylight 1B filter to protect the front element of my lenses, all my photography is natural using available light."

Photographing lightning is a very specialist occupation, and not recommended for the novice as it can be literally a hair-raising and dangerous experience. Nick describes the situation when he took this shot, 'Tempest'.

"The 12th January was a sultry day with all the right atmospheric conditions to trigger the mechanisms which guarantee thunderstorms. The weather bureau had just issued late that afternoon, a severe priority thunderstorm warning.

"Little did I realise how conservative their forecast was to be. It started just after sunset, with thunder squalls coming in from every direction and lasted through to dawn. Tempest was taken that evening. It was quite a surreal,

if not downright dangerous experience photographing the thunderstorms that evening.

"Needless to say, I never got a chance to make it to shelter when this was taken. The storm started to intensify and change direction, heading straight for me. All of a sudden, it was like a switch had been thrown. For three and a half minutes, the lightning was flashing inside the clouds, seen by the streaming effect within the clouds. Then the whole ocean just erupted a couple of kilometres away from me with a cataclysmic explosion which only lasted a couple of seconds.

"I hardly had time to get far enough away from my tripod and into a crouching position when again the sky erupted and the lightning bolts hit the ocean a couple of hundred metres away from me. All these lightning bolts struck at the same time and it felt like a bomb had gone off under me.

"The thunderclap and the lightning flash were simultaneous. I was flash-blinded for a few seconds and I'd thought my eardrums had been perforated. I had severe ringing in my ears for a short while afterwards and it took about half an hour for my hearing to return to normal. After this close encounter, I thought it's about time to pull up stumps and head for the bunker.

"I barely had enough time to get the protective covering over my camera on the tripod before the heavens opened up. By the time I got to my car, I was like a drowned rat and the thunderstorm was right over the top of me with lightning bolts striking the ground about 50 to 100 metres from where I was parked.

Meanwhile, my camera was sitting out in the middle of this mayhem and I was wondering what the hell was happening to it. Fortunately, my camera (and I) survived and I thought this experience would take one heck of a lot of beating."

The circumstances were evidently, from Nick's breath-taking account, quite extreme, and the impact of the final image certainly reflects this. What the shot actually consists of is the cumulative effect of a series of lightning flashes. So in effect, this is a multiple exposure caused by a sequence of tremendous lightning strikes that occurred during the full three and a half minutes that the camera shutter was open.

There are some interesting points to note about the practicalities of working in this kind of setting. If you look at the reflections in the sea water in the centre of the frame, the streaks of lightning are reflected quite clearly as pools of rippling white light on the waves. But on the left of the frame, notice that one of the final lightning strikes to be recorded, gave absolutely no reflection in the water. This apparently puzzling phenomenon actually has a straightforward explanation. It is because there was actually no water in the appropriate place at the exact moment that this particular strike occurred. The natural continuous movement of the waves meant that there was not necessarily any water in position to create a reflection for any one strike, and the result of the ebb and flow is the lack of reflection in this area of the shot.

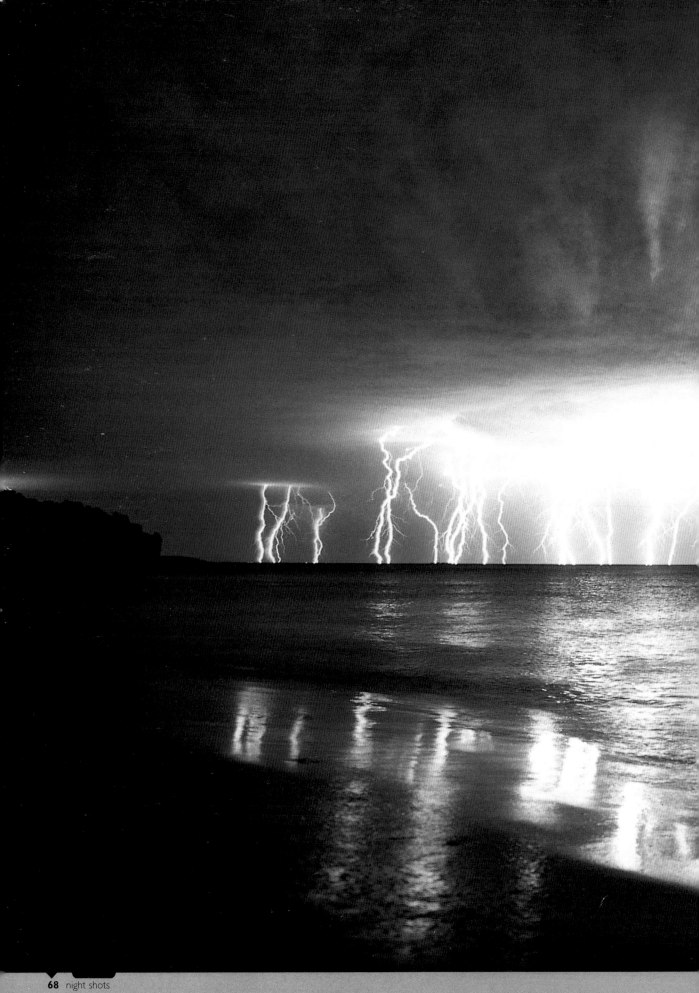

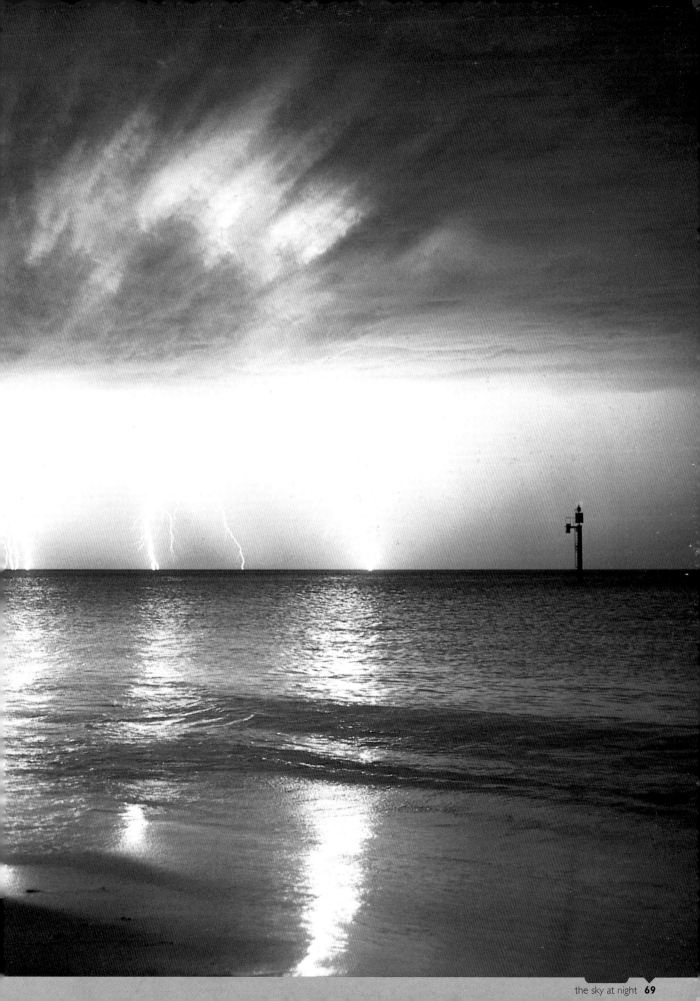

TWILIGHT ZONE

▼

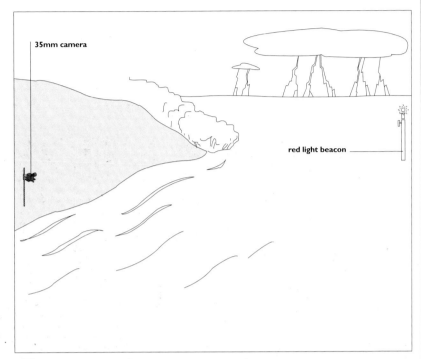

Photographer: **Nick Djordjevic**

Client: **Self-promotion**

Use: **Calendar, fine art prints**

Camera: **Nikon F4**

Lens: **20mm**

Film: **Fuji Velvia**

Exposure: **I hour at f/5.6**

Lighting: **Available light (lightning)**

Props and background: **Ocean Reef, Perth**

THIS IS A VERY GOOD EXAMPLE OF USING CLOUD AS A WIND BAG, I.E. ONE OF THE BIGGEST SOFT BOXES OR REFLECTORS THAT ANYONE CAN EVER USE.

The distinctive green haze is created by the effect of city sodium lighting some distance behind the photographer. The light dispersed through and bounced off an extremely low cloud bank, producing the distinctive coloration of the final image.

The fact that no filtration or after-treatment was used is evident from the details. Look at the red beacon and the streak of white lightning. If a filter had been used these would also have changed colour, which would of course have ruined the effect.

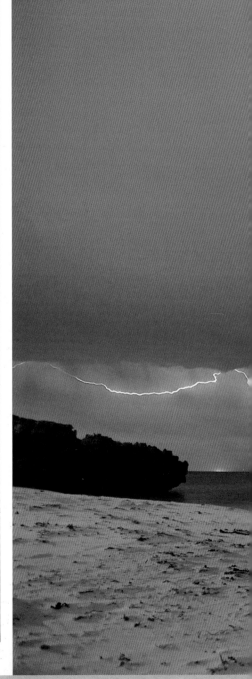

Photographer's comment:

Available as a fine art lithographic poster.

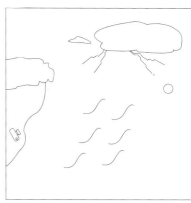

Plan View

ELECTRIC DREAMS

▼

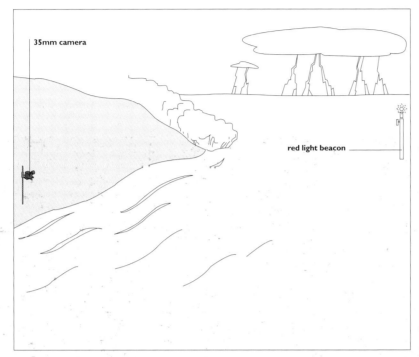

Photographer: **Nick Djordjevic**

Client: **Self-promotion**

Use: **Calendar, fine art prints**

Camera: **Nikon F4**

Lens: **24mm**

Film: **Kodachrome 64**

Exposure: **20 minutes at f/5.6**

Lighting: **Ambient light (lightning)**

Props and background: **Ocean Reef, Perth**

35mm camera

red light beacon

IN CONTRAST TO "TEMPEST", NICK DJORDJEVIC CHOSE IN THIS SHOT TO CAPTURE THE MAGNIFICENCE AND CLARITY OF A SINGLE SPECTACULAR LIGHTNING STRIKE.

While the huge amount of lightning in "Tempest" conjures up the atmosphere of being at the centre of a phenomenal maelstrom, emphasising the awe-inspiring immensity of the storm, there is a quite different visual power to the clear, lone zig-zag of lightning in this shot. Different approaches to basically the same subject matter can give hugely varying results in terms of mood, presence, composition, impact and scale.

Photographer's comment:

Available as a fine art lithographic poster.

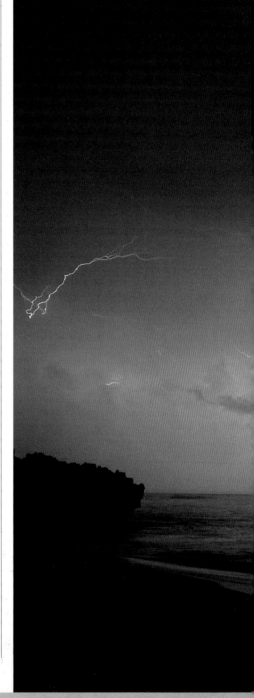

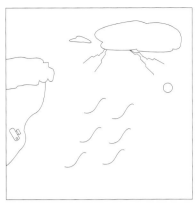

Plan View

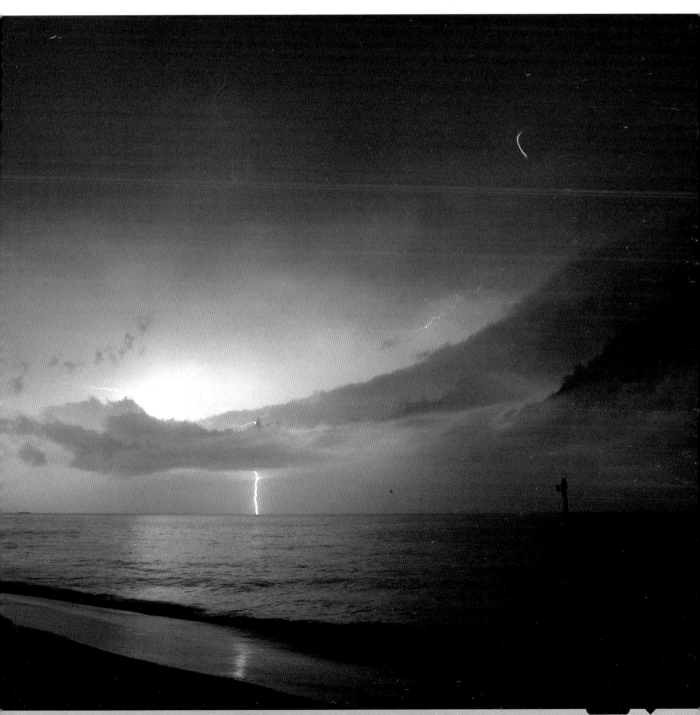

TWICKENHAM RUGBY GROUND

▼

Photographer: **Tim Hawkins**

Client: **Philips Lighting**

Use: **Promotional**

Camera: **4x5 inch**

Lens: **65mm**

Film: **VHC**

Exposure: **1/2 second at f/11 1/2**

Lighting: **Available light**

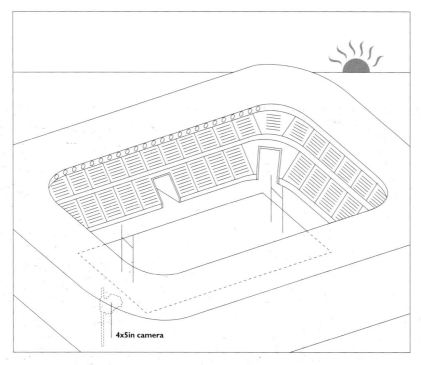

4x5in camera

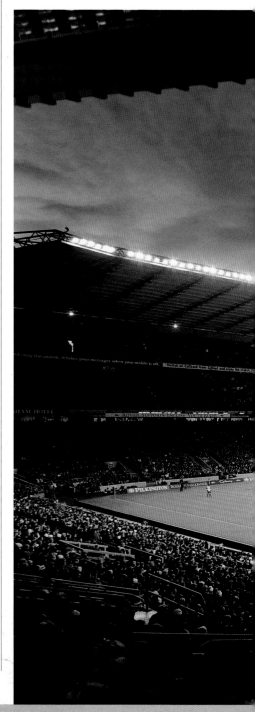

Photographing a rugby stadium raises many considerations for the photographer. Tim Hawkins specialises in night-time photography of illuminated architectural and industrial subjects and knew just how to tackle the challenge. He explains some of the thinking behind this shot.

"This took a year to arrange. You can't wander round with a 4x5 camera so I had to do a recce with the tripod and eventually came up with two agreed locations. When photographing stadia it is far better looking down – it gives better composition and reduces the chances of flare.

"The match was on late at night in winter with the floodlights on for the last half of the match. This type of lighting has a slightly green tint but when printing the negative the lab use a magenta filter to correct for the greenness.

"The set routines in rugby such as scrums and line-outs are good for the photographer because it means the players stand still for long enough not to record as a blur. I could have photographed the stadium empty but it wouldn't be the same as when it is full. Atmosphere can come across with the game, depending on the crowd."

As Tim says, this is a winter night sky. The magenta correction at the printing stage adds to the colour tones and warms up the cool winter lighting, making the picture more inviting.

► By careful planning and by checking weather reports long- and short-term, Tim Hawkins chose an evening which combined a rugby match and a fascinating sky

► With modern technology it is possible to add such elements as sky detail digitally from another source, at a later stage

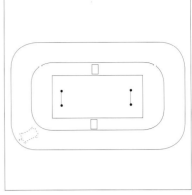

Plan View

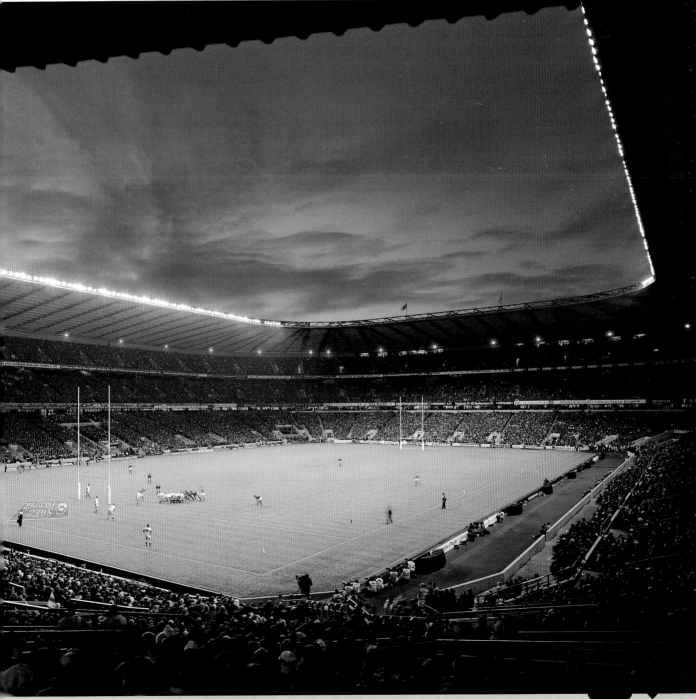

STATUE OF LIBERTY

Photographer: **André Maier**

Use: **Portfolio, exhibition**

Camera: **35mm**

Lens: **200mm**

Film: **Fuji Velvia**

Exposure: **1/60 second at f/2.8**

Lighting: **Available light**

▼

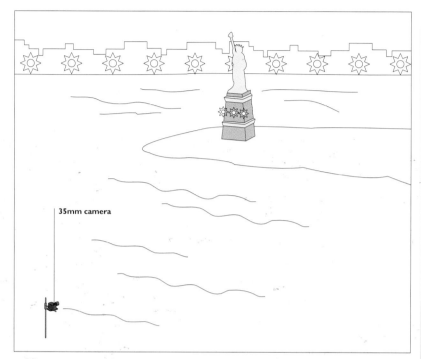

35mm camera

"**N**O FILTERS, JUST THE REGULAR SUNSET AT THE RIGHT TIME AND ANGLE (THAT IS, A LOT OF WAITING AND MANY DAYS OF RETURNING!)" SAYS ANDRÉ MAIER.

This sums up the success of a fresh image of a familiar subject. Identifying a good vantage point takes research and lots of looking; and waiting for just the right moment takes both patience and a watchful eye.

The "regular sunset" gives a marvellous deep, rich red glow, throwing the well-known figure of the Statue of Liberty into bold silhouette, with just the lights on the crown, torch and plinth providing some contrast with the sheer blackness of the shape. The city lights to either side give balance to the composition and provide a sense of scale and proportion.

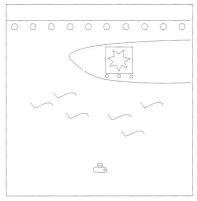

Plan View

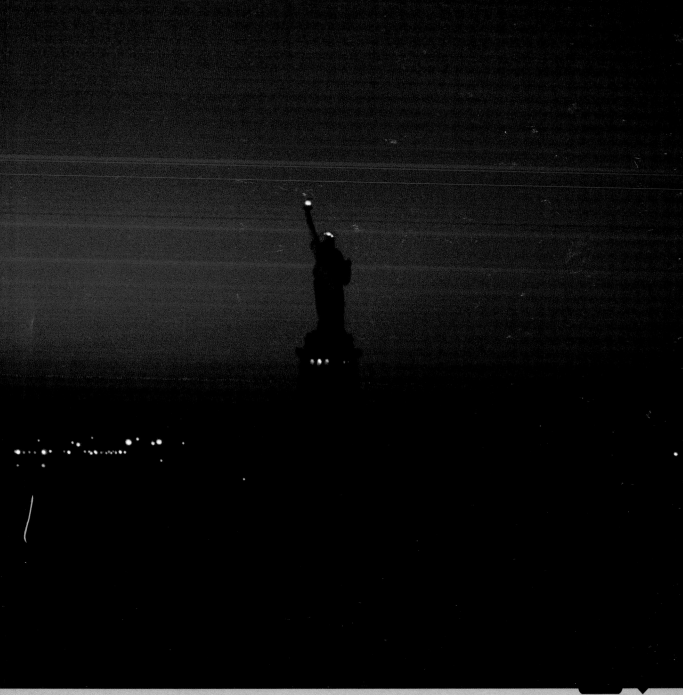

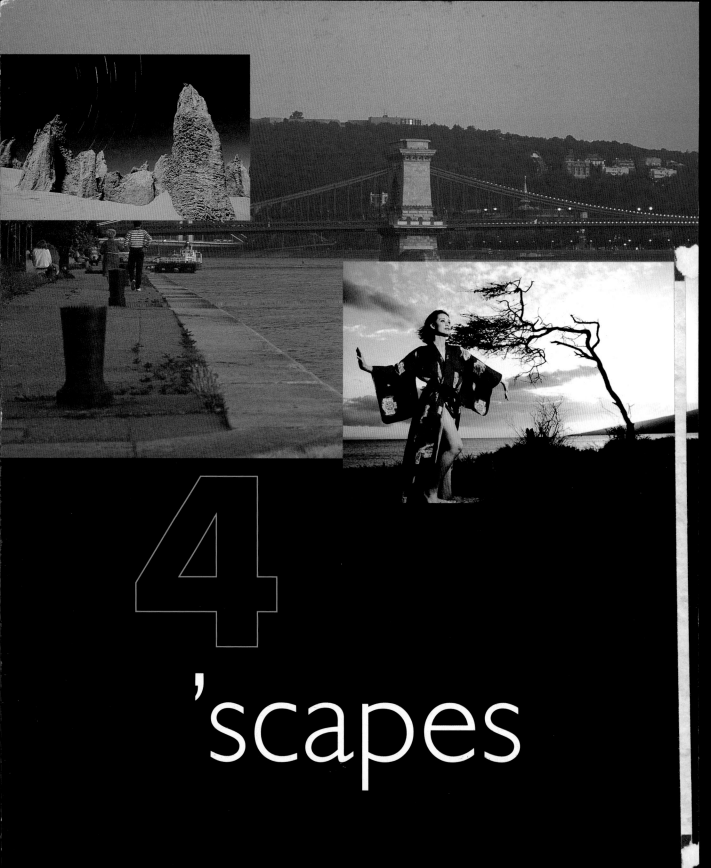

4

'scapes

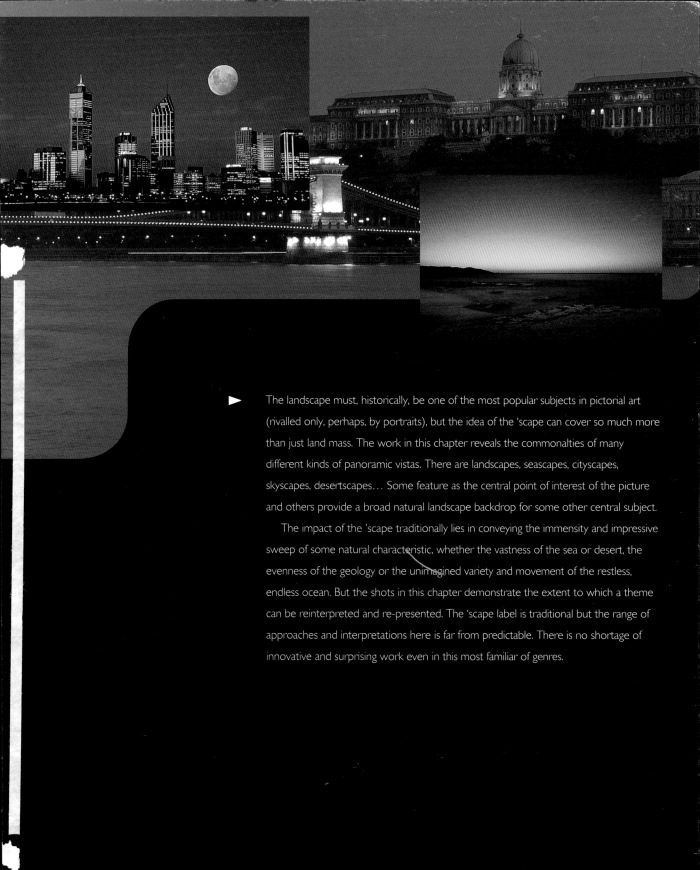

The landscape must, historically, be one of the most popular subjects in pictorial art (rivalled only, perhaps, by portraits), but the idea of the 'scape can cover so much more than just land mass. The work in this chapter reveals the commonalties of many different kinds of panoramic vistas. There are landscapes, seascapes, cityscapes, skyscapes, desertscapes… Some feature as the central point of interest of the picture and others provide a broad natural landscape backdrop for some other central subject.

The impact of the 'scape traditionally lies in conveying the immensity and impressive sweep of some natural characteristic, whether the vastness of the sea or desert, the evenness of the geology or the unimagined variety and movement of the restless, endless ocean. But the shots in this chapter demonstrate the extent to which a theme can be reinterpreted and re-presented. The 'scape label is traditional but the range of approaches and interpretations here is far from predictable. There is no shortage of innovative and surprising work even in this most familiar of genres.

Photographer: **Patricia Novoa**

Client: **Personal work**

Use: **Exhibition**

Assistant: **Luis Gutierrez**

Camera: **6x17cm**

Lens: **105mm**

Film: **Kodak Ektachrome**

Exposure: **45 seconds at f/45**

Lighting: **Moonlight and tungsten**

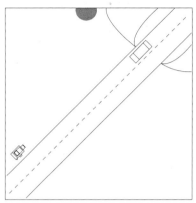

Plan View

RUMBO AL NORTE

▼

THIS IS AN ARCHETYPAL LONG EXPOSURE, IN THE PERFECT SETTING TO SHOW OFF THE TECHNIQUE. PATRICIA NOVOA HAS COMBINED AN INCREDIBLE LANDSCAPE, A WIDE PANORAMA AND AN ENDLESSLY LONG STRAIGHT ROAD, WITH THE JOURNEY OF THE LONE TRAVELLER INDICATED BY THE STREAK OF LIGHT FROM THE CAR HEADLAMPS CUTTING ACROSS THE TWILIGHT DESERT.

To realise this picture, the photographer had to wait for a long time on the edge of the highway, until seeing a car on the horizon approaching with its lights on. The 45-second exposure records not only the movement of the car but also the slight movement of the moon in the top left of the frame. The landscape is lit purely by moonlight and the last traces of light in the evening sky, giving a slight amount of graduation and residual yellow glow from the long-past sunset.

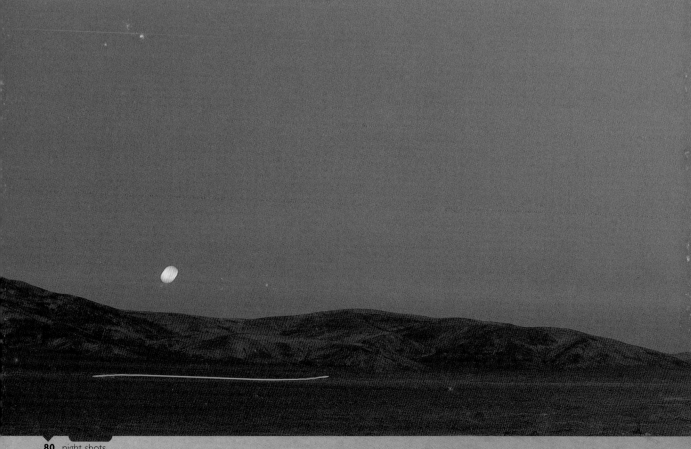

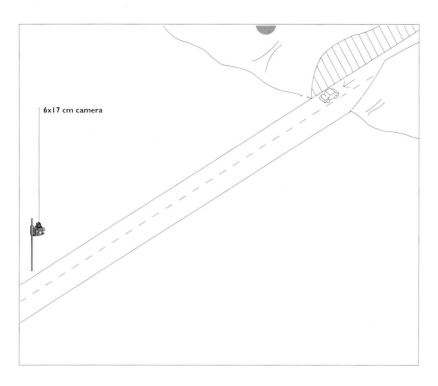

6x17 cm camera

► It is important that the car is approaching the camera rather than going away from it as a streak of red light from rear lights would have given a completely different look

► In a very exposed environment, a windshield may be needed to protect the camera from wind rock

DANTE'S BEACH

▼

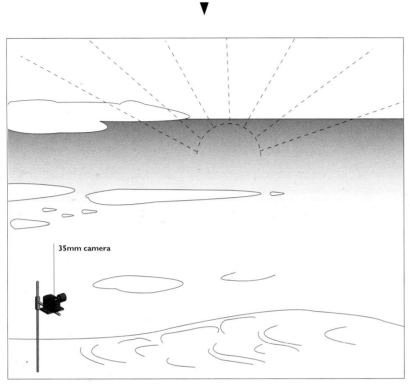

Photographer: **Nick Djordjevic**

Client: **Self-promotion**

Use: **Calendar, fine art prints**

Camera: **35mm**

Lens: **24mm**

Film: **Fuji Velvia 50 ASA**

Exposure: **30 minutes at f/8**

Lighting: **Available light**

THE HALLMARK FEATURE OF NICK DJORDJEVIC'S REMARKABLE AND DISTINCTIVE WORK IS THAT HE DOES NOT USE FILTERS, PRINTING MANIPULATION OR DIGITAL MANIPULATION TO ACHIEVE THE MAGNIFICENT AND EXTRAORDINARY COLOURS OF HIS SHOTS. ONLY AMBIENT LIGHT IS USED, AND WHAT YOU SEE REALLY IS WHAT HE GOT. HIS WORK IS A CASE IN POINT OF UNDERSTANDING THE LIGHT AVAILABLE, AND MAKING THE MOST OF IT.

There are two main contrasting areas in the way the sea has recorded. The small puddles of water in the foreground are sharp because they are static – although there is an element of *trompe d'oeil* in that the undulations in the sand give the impression that we are looking at small waves rippling up the beach.

The main area of the sea in the mid-ground of the shot records as slightly soft because of the continuous movement of the waves during the 30-minute exposure. The contrast between these two areas, one part so sharp and the other so soft, adds to the surreal feel of the image overall.

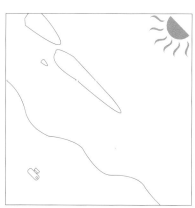

Plan View

Photographer: **Mike Károly**

Client: **Self-promotion**

Use: **Calendar**

Art director: **Mike Károly**

Camera: **4x5cm**

Lens: **135mm Sinaron**

Film: **Agfachrome 100**

Exposure: **Dual exposure; see text**

Lighting: **Available light**

Props and background: **Chains Bridge, Budapest, strong tripod, easy fishing-stool, a good book and patience**

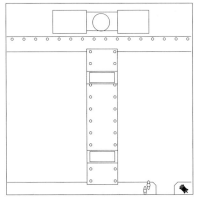

Plan View

DAY AND NIGHT

▼

THIS SHOT IS A DOUBLE EXPOSURE. THE FIRST EXPOSURE AT 1/60 SECOND WAS TAKEN AT ABOUT 6 O'CLOCK IN THE AFTERNOON TO PRODUCE THE LEFT SIDE OF THE FRAME. THE RIGHT SIDE OF THE LENS WAS MASKED BY A COKIN B346 FILTER FOR THIS FIRST STAGE. THE SHUTTER SPEED USED WAS CHOSEN TO FREEZE THE MOTION OF THE PEOPLE AND BOAT IN VIEW TO THE LEFT.

The second exposure was taken more than two hours later, this time with the left side of the lens masked. At this time, the bridge lights had been turned on as night had fallen. This second exposure was for 6 seconds as the conditions were so much darker. One result of this long exposure is that the movement of the river water records as a blur in contrast with the sharp detail of the water to the left, adding interest to the final image.

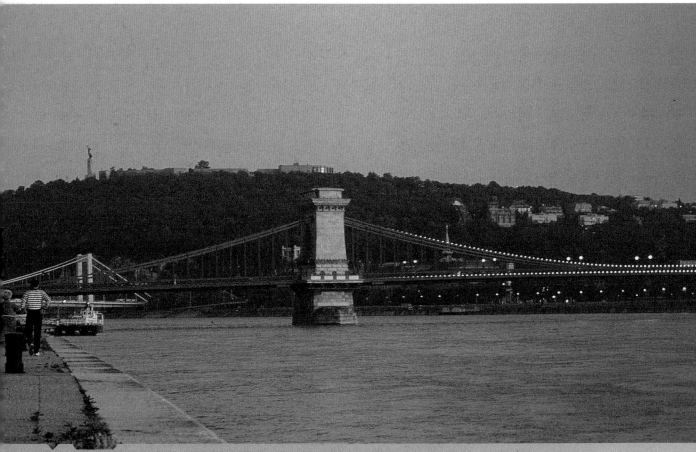

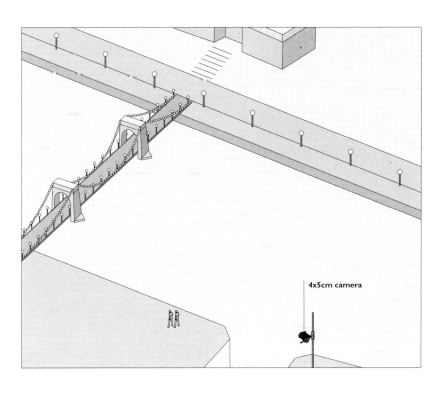

4x5cm camera

► It is very important when physically turning the filter to be absolutely sure not to move the camera at all

► The filter must be moved precisely through 180 degrees to ensure that no part of the film is inadvertently exposed twice

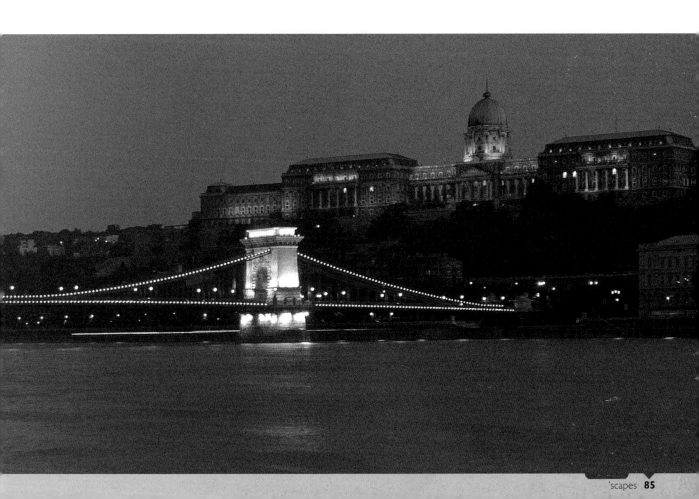

POLYNESIAN FIRE DANCE

▼

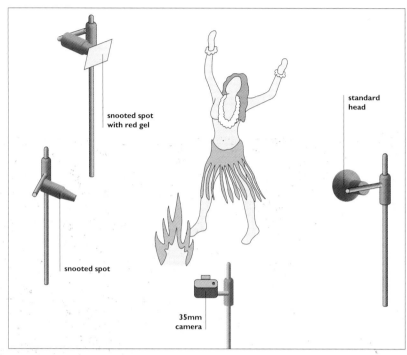

snooted spot
with red gel

standard
head

snooted spot

35mm
camera

Photographer: **Tim Orden**

Client: **Personal work**

Use: **Stock**

Model: **Sunmoon Perrault**

Assistants: **Sean, Kenji**

Make-up: **Donna Orden**

Camera: **35mm**

Lens: **50mm**

Film: **Kodak Ektachrome 400**

Exposure: **Not recorded**

Lighting: **Available light (twilight and fire) plus electronic flash, 3 heads**

Props and background: **Hawaiian beach**

"I WANTED TO CREATE A PICTURE WITH ALL THE ELEMENTS OF AN EXCITING NIGHT SHOT," SAYS TIM ORDEN. "IT HAD TO HAVE: (I) A GREAT SUNSET; (II) FLASH; (III) FIRE LIGHT; AND (IV) REAR CURTAIN SHUTTER. WITH THESE AND OTHER PHOTOGRAPHIC VARIABLES I WAS SET. WE HEADED DOWN TO A SECLUDED BEACH IN WAILEA WHERE THERE WOULD BE NO PROBLEM WITH BUILDING A FIRE ON THE BEACH. WE WERE LUCKY, THE USUAL TRADE CLOUDS OVER MAKENA WERE NOT SO THICK. THIS MEANT WE WERE GOING TO HAVE A SUNSET.

"The fire was blazing at first. We had a good supply of lighter fuel to keep it up to 'photo intensity'. Unfortunately, every time my assistant squirted fuel onto the flames, I was choking from smoke and fumes. As the night became darker, the exposures became longer and the light from the fire became the more dominant light source. With the long exposures there was subject movement to deal with. I chose to set the N90s to rear curtain flash. This made for logical 'ghost trails' from the subject movement."

Tim used a red light behind the fire to add a tinge of colour to the flames from the rear, along with a standard head for back lighting the fire. A boomed main light lit the model from directly in front.

Photographer's comment:

The first order of business was to convince everyone to work for as little as possible since I had no client for this shot.. I couldn't have done it without Sean and Kenji assisting and Donna on styling and make-up, and of course, one of my favourite models, Sunmoon.

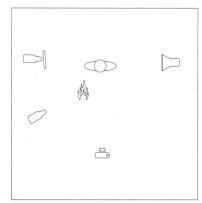

Plan View

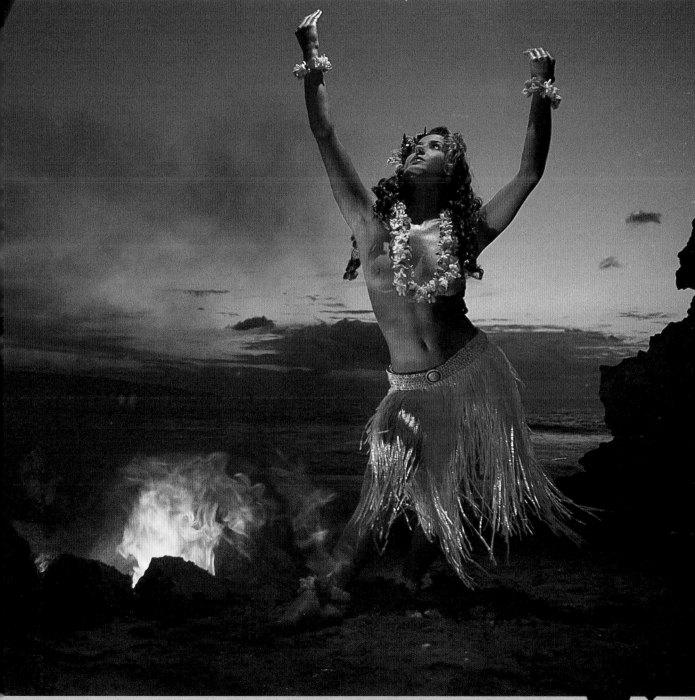

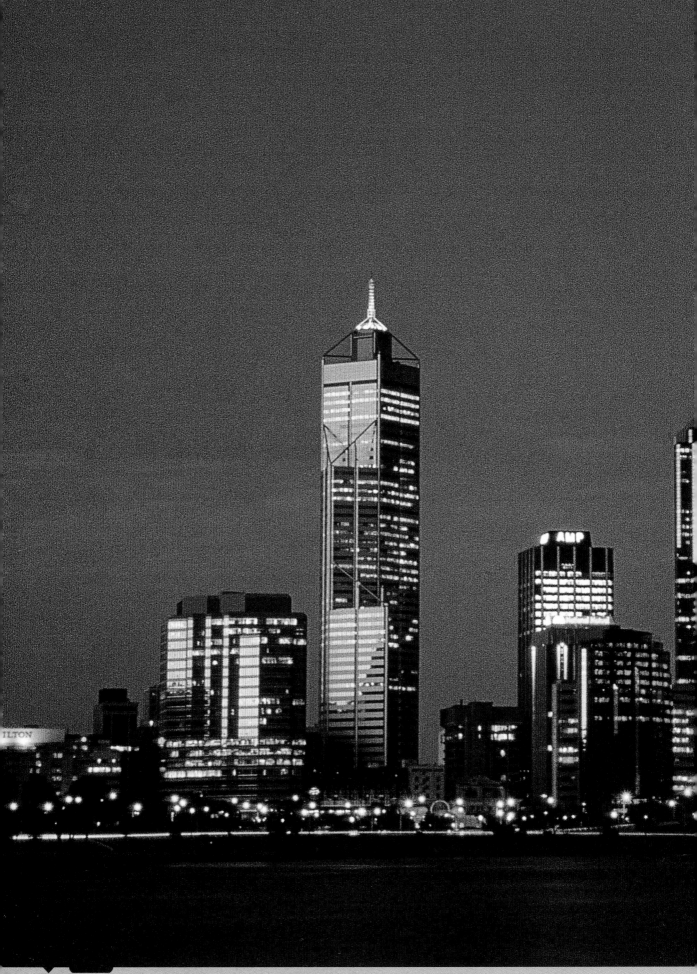

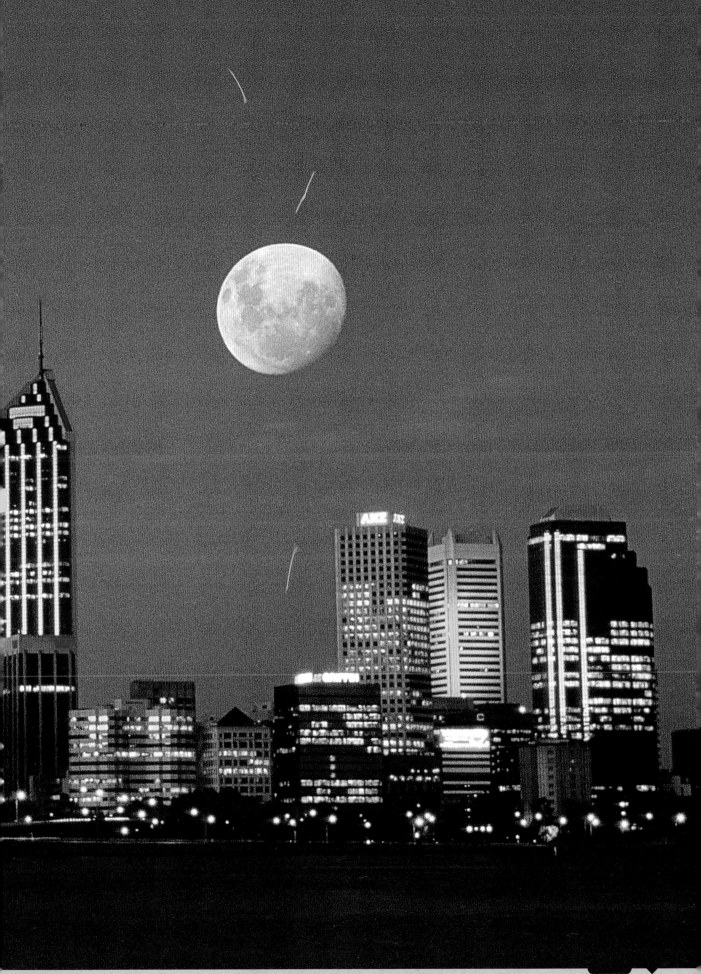

Photographer: **Nick Djordjevic**

Client: **Personal work**

Use: **Calendar; self-promotion**

Camera: **35mm**

Lens: **80–200mm with 1.6 TC**

Film: **Fuji Velvia 50 ASA**

Exposure: **Double exposure; see text**

Lighting: **Available light**

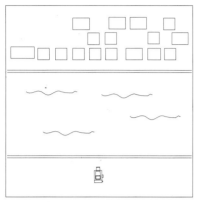

First Exposure

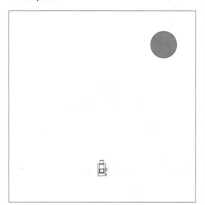

Second Exposure

► *When making a double exposure on 35mm it is important to have a good mental image of the initial exposure, and possibly a sketch on paper, to ensure correct positioning of the secondary image*

► *If a larger format is being used it is helpful to mark the ground glass with a chinagraph pencil to achieve correct positioning*

T W I L I G H T   M O O N

▼

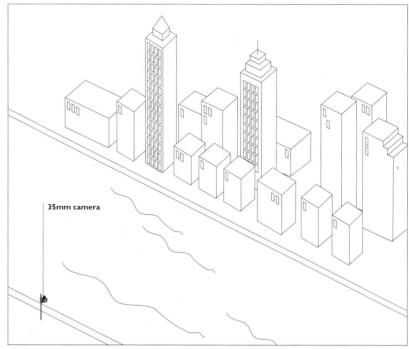

35mm camera

The CITYSCAPE WAS TAKEN USING AN 80–200MM LENS SET AT THE 80MM END OF THE RANGE WITH AN EXPOSURE OF 40 SECONDS AT F/8.

It was important that there was very little ambient light from the lights in the buildings, and that there was no moon in the sky. From a compositional point of view, the strong, parallel verticals of the city buildings and bold horizontal divide between city and water are crucial. The straight lines all contrast with the perfect circle of the moon, put into place later on, by means of double exposure on the same frame of film.

The moon was shot using the 200mm end of the same lens with a 1.6 teleconverter at an exposure of 1/125 second at f/8.

Photographer: **Tim Orden**

Client: **Personal work**

Use: **Stock**

Model: **Monica**

Camera: **35mm**

Lens: **50mm**

Film: **Fuji Velvia rated at 100 ISO, cross-processed in C41 chemistry**

Exposure: **Not recorded**

Lighting: **Electronic flash: 1 head plus ambient light**

Props and background: **Tree, nature reserve**

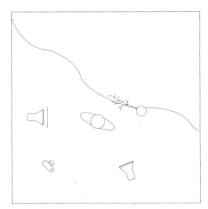

Plan View

▼

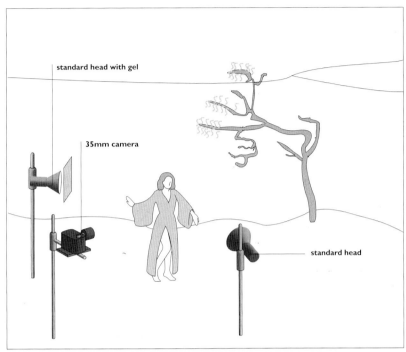

standard head with gel

35mm camera

standard head

"**T**HIS WAS A PORTRAIT/GLAMOUR EXPERIMENT," SAYS TIM ORDEN. "I HAD SEEN THE WIND-BLOWN TREES FROM THE HIGHWAY. THEY REMINDED ME OF JAPANESE PAINTINGS.

Hence, I got the kimono from a make-up/stylist and proceeded to emulate the style of Japanese paintings. Like so many of our Hawaiian island residents, Monica, the model, is of mixed ancestry, a mix of European and Asian."

Following his usual technique with sunsets, Tim set the aperture to the main flash and then set the meter according to the reflected zone 5 reading of the sky (by simply pointing the camera to the sky and setting the shutter speed accordingly). The surreal feel of the final image comes from the cross-processing, giving the characteristic heightened contrast (for example in the cloud formations) and enriched intensity of colour, especially in the early evening sky and the kimono.

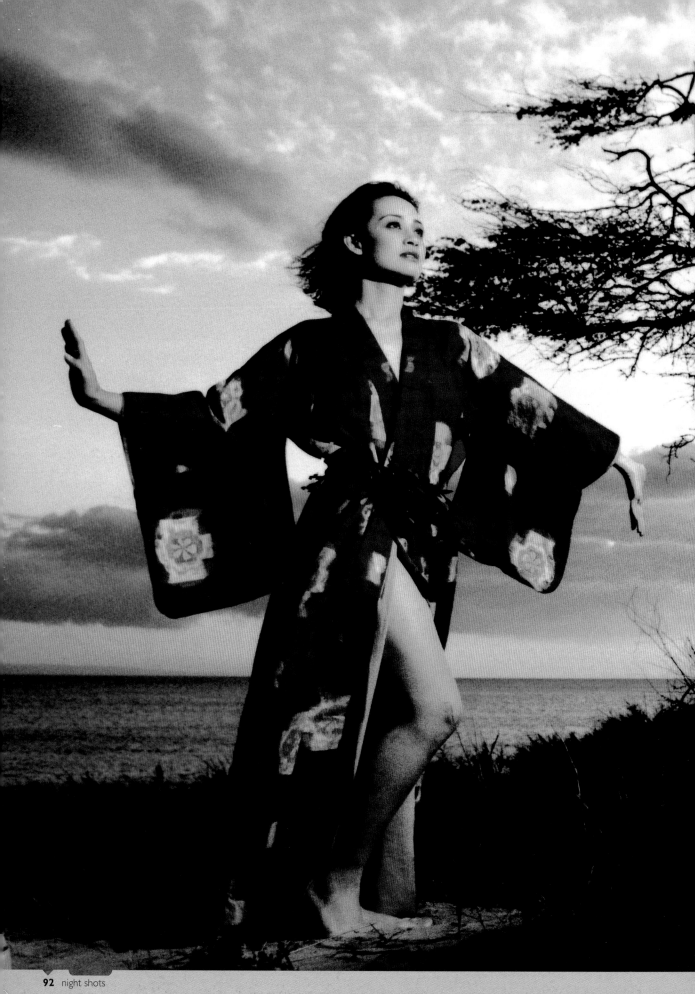

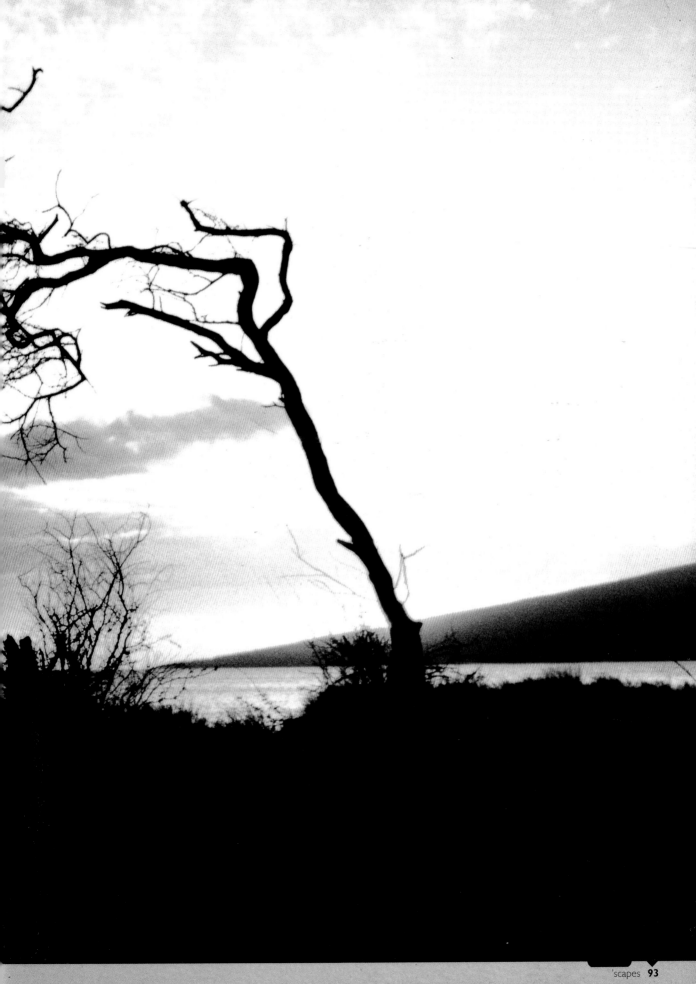

SENTINELS

▼

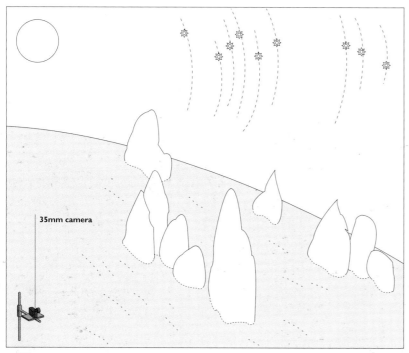

Photographer: **Nick Djordjevic**

Client: **Personal work**

Use: **Self-promotion**

Camera: **35mm**

Lens: **20mm**

Film: **Kodak Select 50 ASA**

Exposure: **I hour at f/5.6**

Lighting: **Available light**

35mm camera

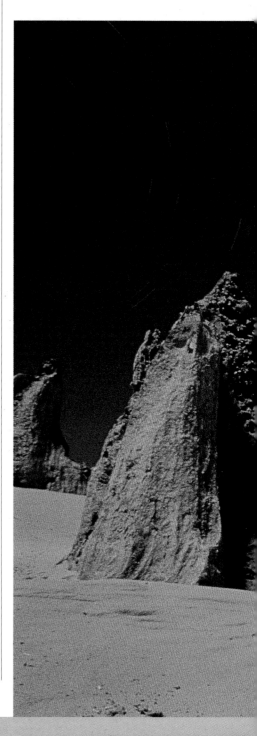

THESE FASCINATING ARCS OF LIGHT, TRACED ACROSS THE SKY, ARE IN FACT STAR TRAILS, CREATED BY TAKING AN EXTREMELY LONG EXPOSURE SO THAT THE APPARENT MOVEMENT OF THE STARS (ACTUALLY THE MOVEMENT OF THE EARTH) THROUGH THE NIGHT SKY RECORD AS CURVES ACROSS THE SKY.

Nick Djordjevic left the shutter open for a full hour for this shot. Even longer exposures can give full circles of star trails in the right conditions. For such an effect, ideally, the camera would need to pointing directly up into a starry sky with very little other ambient light.

The natural variations in the colour of the light from the stars, not generally discernable by the naked eye, turn out to be distinctly contrasting when captured on a long exposure of this kind.

► *The colours are enhanced here by cross-processing*

► *Choose a location without light pollution from city lights for the best results*

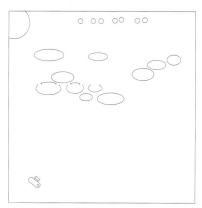

Plan View

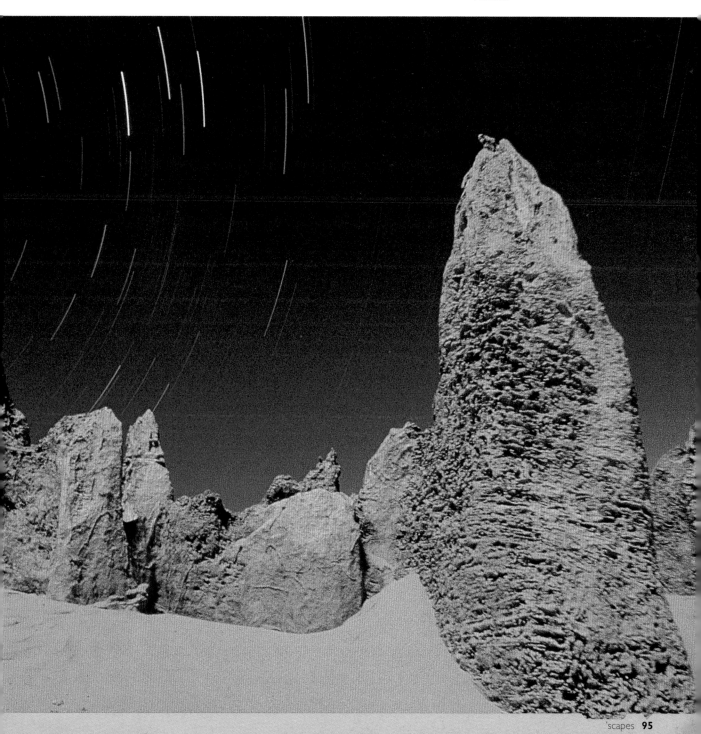

BIG BEN

▼

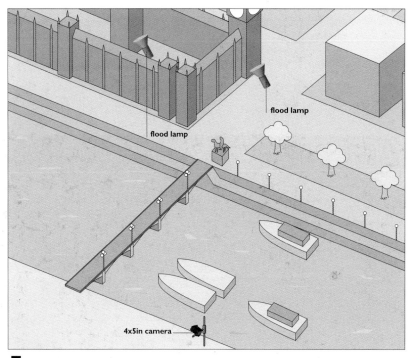

Photographer: **Tim Hawkins**

Client: **Philips**

Use: **Promotional**

Camera: **4x5 inch**

Lens: **150mm standard lens**

Film: **Kodak VHC 100**

Exposure: **1 second at f/16**

Lighting: **Available light**

Props and background: **Houses of Parliament**

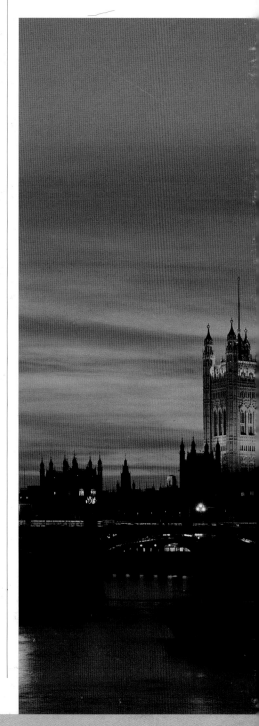

THIS PAIR OF SHOTS DEMONSTRATES THE IMPORTANCE OF TIMING AND THE DIFFERENCE THAT A FEW MINUTES CAN MAKE AT DUSK WHEN CRUCIAL AMBIENT LIGHT IS FADING QUICKLY.

These two shots were taken 15 minutes apart, as the time on the clock face shows. Although there was more ambient light available for the first, there is greater intensity of colour and richness in the second. This is because in the first shot, the relatively bright sky outweighs the foreground, throwing the building more into silhouette. As the sky darkens, however, in the second shot, the lighting on the building becomes more apparent. There is what Tim Hawkins describes as a "magic moment" when the sky darkens just enough for the balance of light and interest to shift onto the building; a moment that lasts, by his estimation, for about five minutes only – if that. Timing is all-important.

Notice that the lighting on one clock face is brighter than the other. This is because Philips had installed special lamps on one side, which were brighter, more efficient, using only a quarter of the power, and long-lasting, with a life-span of some 20 years. The purpose of the shot was to demonstrate the difference between the old and new bulbs.

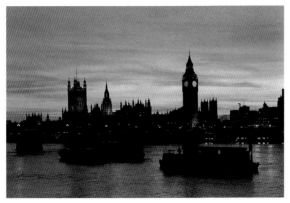

First Exposure

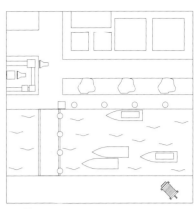

Plan View

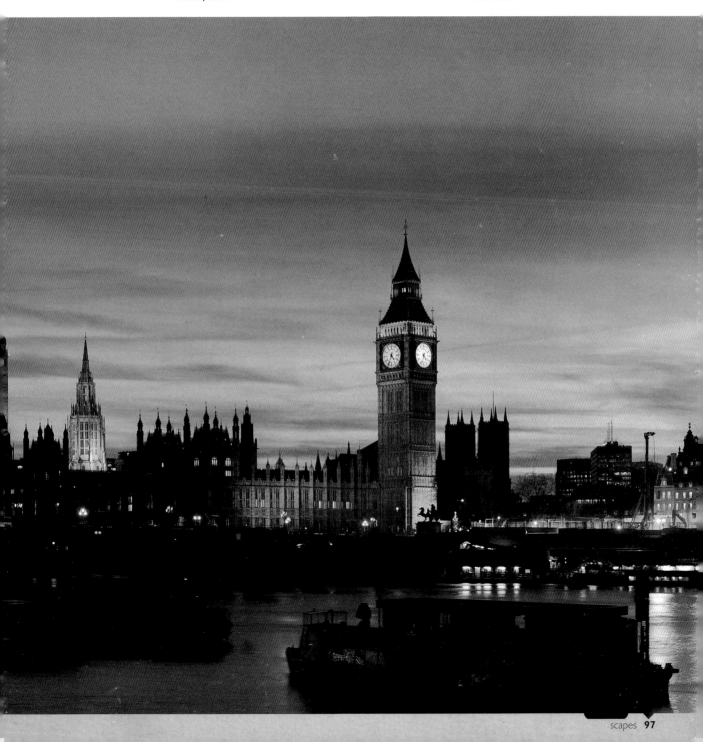

CITY STORM

Photographer: **Michael Bath**

Client: **Personal work**

Use: **Calendar, magazine, Web page**

Camera: **35mm**

Lens: **50mm**

Film: **Kodak Pro Gold 100**

Exposure: **35 seconds at f/4; 25 seconds at f/2.8**

Lighting: **City lights, lightning**

▼

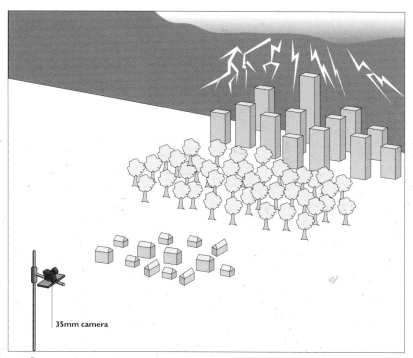

35mm camera

"**A** VERY ELECTRICALLY ACTIVE BUT SLOW-MOVING STORM WAS A GREAT SUBJECT," SAYS MICHAEL BATH. "THE FIRST SHOW WAS A SINGLE FLASH OF LIGHTNING, WHILE THE SECOND HAS TWO DISTINCT FLASHES WITHIN THE EXPOSURE TIME.

"Because of the frequency of the lightning I was able to press the shutter, wait for the lightning, then release it. I was looking for roughly 30-second exposures so as to capture the entire storm structure and colour from the city lights. The storm was located directly over Sydney CBD, approximately 40 kilometres away."

The presence of the trees and buildings on the horizon is an important factor in the success of the final image, giving context and scale, adding to a strong sense of the immensity of the storm and its phenomenal power in relation to human existence below.

The interesting effect to note here is the extraordinary back lighting of the clouds by the flash of lightning. As with studio-created clouds of vapour from smoke machines, back lighting gives good definition of the form of the clouds, lighting the clouds themselves, as opposed to front lighting when the clouds tend to diffuse the light and lose detail of the cloud form.

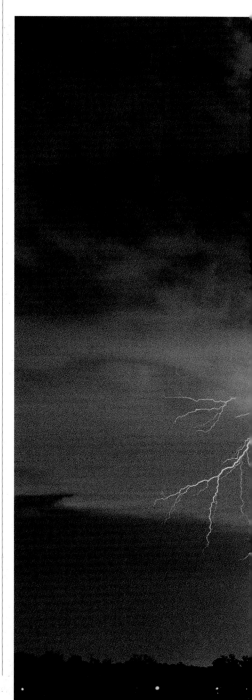

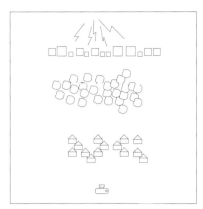

Plan View

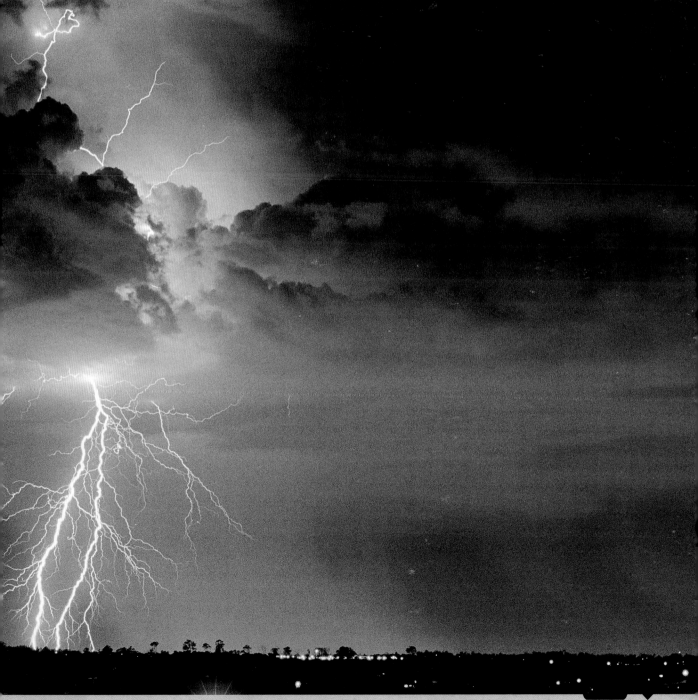

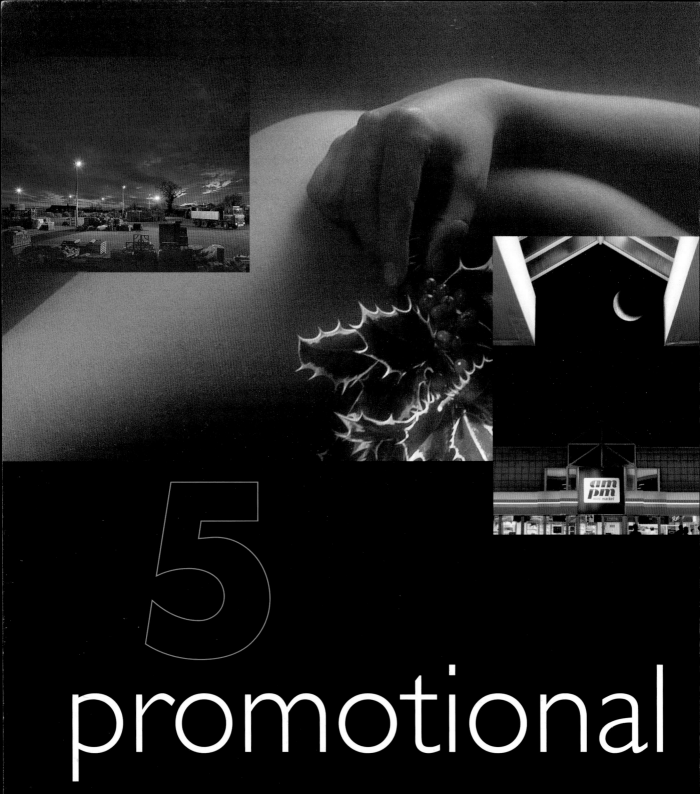

5
promotional

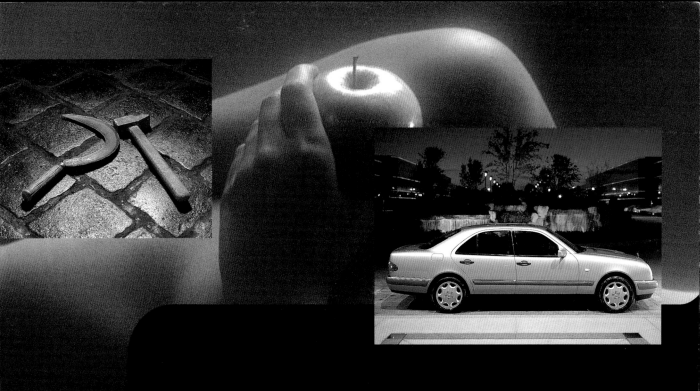

The allure of the night is a natural draw for many advertisers and photographers. Depending on the image of the product, the potentially romantic, dramatic or moody associations of night can be just what is required to create the right associations. The first consideration for the photographer is whether to arrange the shoot at an outdoor night location, or whether to create a simulation of night in a studio. There are strong arguments for favouring each option and, interestingly, the split between studio and location shots featured in this chapter is roughly half and half.

The outdoor night-time location has in its favour the sheer scale of the setting (for example the lodge house in Harry Lomax's shot on page 112-113 - not readily rebuilt in a studio!), excitement, absolute authenticity and such elements ready for exploiting such as passing car light trails, ambient city lighting, the night sky, moonlight, and so on.

Ironically, some of the exact same elements can be construed as arguments for arranging the shoot in a studio. Uncontrollable ambient city lighting may be the last thing the shot needs and the photographer may prefer to create the moon and stars in conditions where they can be placed exactly where they are needed. For a promotional shot, capturing the product in a prominent and recognisable form is a central consideration and for a portable product the studio may offer the best resources for showing it off to best advantage. Obviously, when the product is a building or a concept, the practical considerations will be different. The role of the photographer is to weigh up the advantages of all the options available for each individual case.

IKEA HAMMER AND SICKLE

Photographer: **Mike Károly**

Client: **Ikea**

Use: **Magazine advertisement**

Assistant: **Wife, Eva**

Creative Director: **François Jaglin /F/ Dassas**

Art director: **Patrick Walhain /F/ Dassas, Maria Csöpi Jancsó /H/ JMM**

Stylist: **Jean Michel Ciochetti /F/ Dassas**

Other: **Zoltán Kószegi /H/ Ikea**

Camera: **4x5 inch**

Lens: **210mm**

Film: **Fujichrome 100 ASA**

Exposure: **Double exposure**

Lighting: **Electronic flash, fluorescent strips**

Props and background: **Street with basalt paving stones**

▼

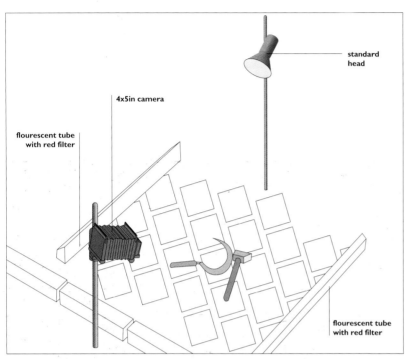

standard head

4x5in camera

flourescent tube with red filter

flourescent tube with red filter

THE SET-UP CAN BE SEEN IN THE THUMBNAIL IMAGE BELOW, SHOWING THE PREPARATION OF THE SUBJECT AREA AND THE POSITIONING OF THE FLUORESCENT STRIPS.

Mike Károly first undertook studio tests, but the final image was shot on location in a street. A site was chosen with good access to a mains electricity supply, actually outside an all-night shop which provided some ambient light for the shoot. Two cars were parked at either end of the subject area and an area of approximately 2 square metres of street paving stones were cleaned and scrubbed with cooking oil to give a gleaming wet-look surface. Finally, the hammer and sickle were put in position and the lighting was arranged, consisting of red fluorescent strips on either side of the subject and a standard head with reflector and barn doors to the rear, 1.8 metres in height.

For the first exposure, the angle of the flash head gives a highlight reflection area on the stones and picks out the upper surfaces of the tools, revealing the range of textures and throwing hard shadows to the front. For the second exposure Mike Károly used a strong red monochrome filter in front of the lens to enhance the effect of the two fluorescent strips with red gels on the nearside edges of the subject.

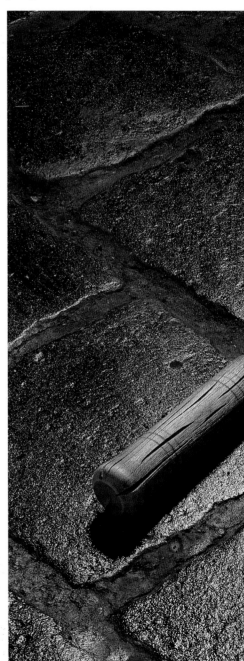

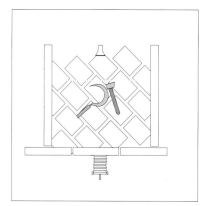

Plan View

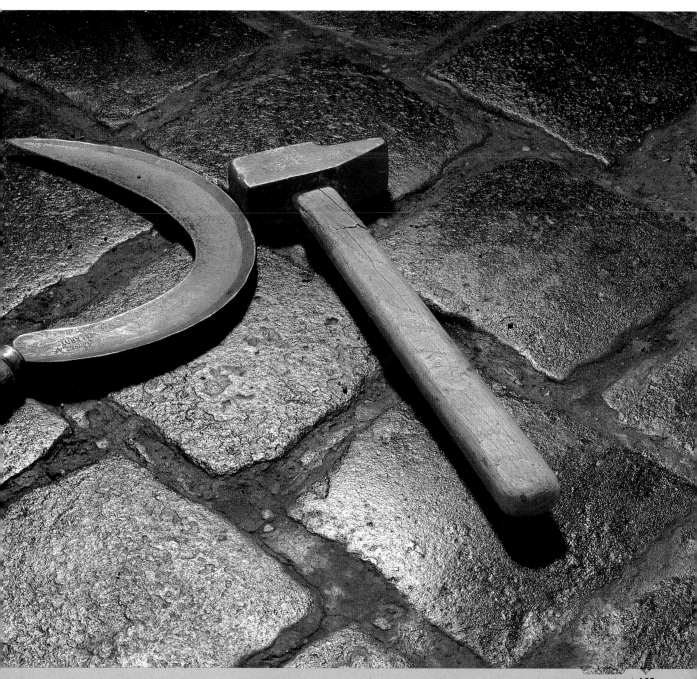

SECURITY LIGHTING

Photographer: **Harry Lomax**

Client: **T. H. White Ltd**

Use: **Editorial**

Camera: **4x5 inch**

Lens: **65mm**

Film: **Kodak VHC**

Exposure: **8 seconds at f/16**

Lighting: **Available light**

Props and background: **Builders' yard**

▼

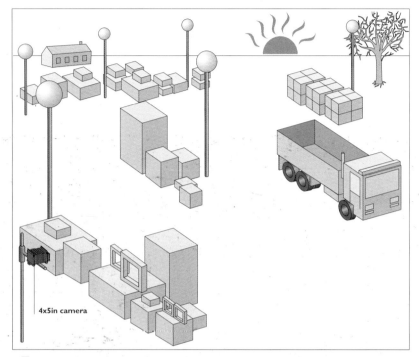

4x5in camera

For this location shot, the yard floodlighting was obviously already in place and not able to be moved. The challenge for the photographer was therefore to work within these parameters and find the best position in relation to the lighting available to give the required end result.

The lorry was carefully positioned to capture the even sheet of light on its side (coming from the lamp nearest the camera which appears in the frame as the third lamp from the left). The light on the front of the lorry comes from a lamp out of view to the right.

The choice of shooting on negative film was to exploit the nature of reciprocity failure on VHC as the film tends to shift into magenta. Thus the ambient lighting (green) becomes neutral (relatively) and an otherwise dull sky gets colour.

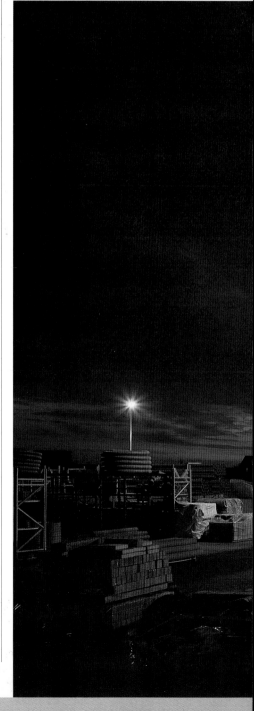

► It is important to know the characteristics of different film stocks and use them as appropriate

► Polaroid tests cannot be relied upon to give an accurate indication of colour renditioning on other films stocks. Experimentation is the best way to learn how different light sources record on different stocks

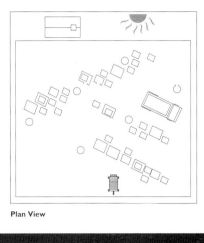

Plan View

MERCEDES BENZ

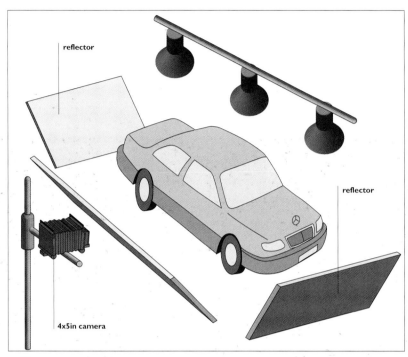

Photographer: **Ben Lagunas/BLAK Productions**

Client: **Mercedes Benz**

Model: **E320!**

Assistants: **Luis Lazcano/Isaias Lagunas**

Art director: **Bianca Mayagoitia**

Camera: **4x5 inch**

Lens: **150mm Schneider**

Film: **Kodak EPP**

Exposure: **7 seconds at f/11**

Lighting: **Available light and flash**

Location: **The airport, Sacsa's FBO building**

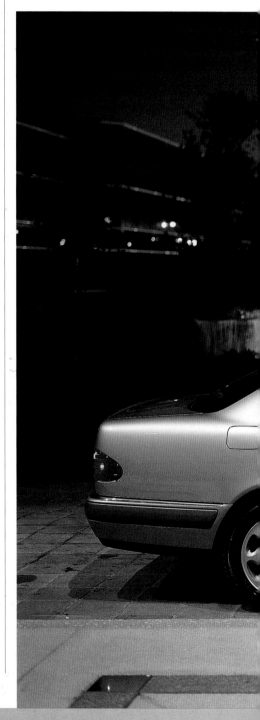

THE RIGHT BACKGROUND IS THE STARTING POINT FOR A SUCCESSFUL AND STRIKING IMAGE. NOTICE HOW THE SHAPE OF THE WATERFALL ECHOES THE OUTLINE OF THE CAR, EVEN DOWN TO THE DETAIL OF A WHEEL SHAPE AT THE APPROPRIATE EQUIVALENT POINT, AND A RISING BOULDER AT THE END OF THE WALL TO IMITATE THE FIGUREHEAD DETAIL ON THE CAR'S BONNET. THE SYMMETRY OF THE SETTING ALSO CONTRIBUTES, GIVING BALANCE TO THE COMPOSITION.

Three standard heads are suspended on a lighting rig over the near edge of the car. This gives good highlights on the upturned surfaces, with the bounce below and to the front sending in spill light to the lower panels directly facing the camera and, more importantly, ensuring that any reflections in the car are only of white light. It also eliminates the possibility of any distracting reflections of people, camera equipment and so on.

The car's own lights are turned on, giving a pool of light on the ground in front of the car, and surprisingly little red at the back. This is managed by careful positioning of the reflector which controls the amount of red spill to some extent.

Photographer's comment:

The client wanted a "natural look" for the picture so we decided to support a 70 per cent on available light and wait for the best moment for the dusk light.

► Lighting rigs can be hired at an outlet near you!

► One possibility for controlling the red glow from a rear car light in this situation would be to use black masking tape over the back-facing part of the lamp, leaving just the visible, camera-facing area exposed and aglow

► Be very aware of reflections when working with a highly reflective subject and make sure you only have those that you want

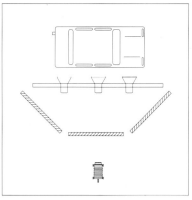

Plan View

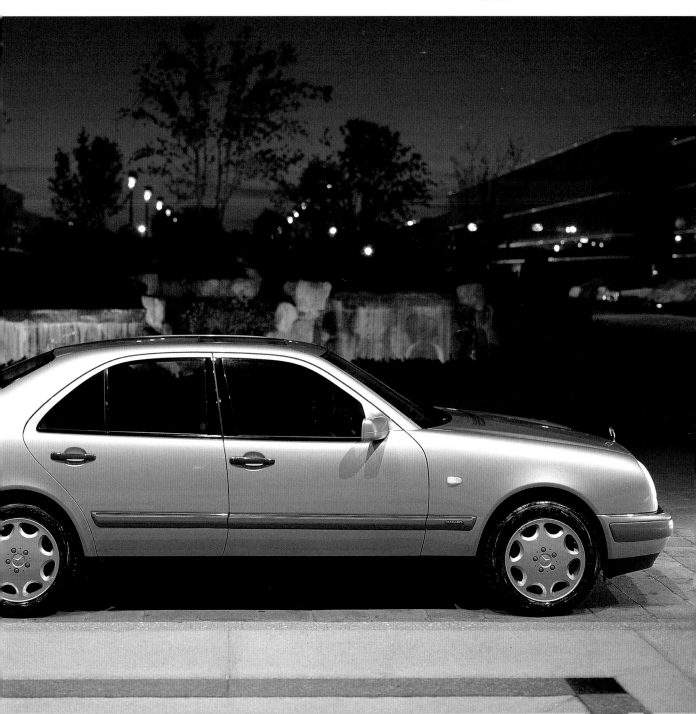

MARIO VALENTINO SHOE

Photographer: **Salvio Parisi**

Client: **Mario Valentino Shoes**

Use: **Editorial**

Model: **Angie Politte**

Assistant: **Chicca Fusco**

Art director: **Adriano Caramenti**

Hair and make-up: **Anna Alliata**

Stylist: **Marco Meininger**

Camera: **4x5 inch**

Lens: **180mm**

Film: **Kodak Ektachrome 64T**

Exposure: **1/250 second at f/11**

Lighting: **Electronic flash, 3 heads**

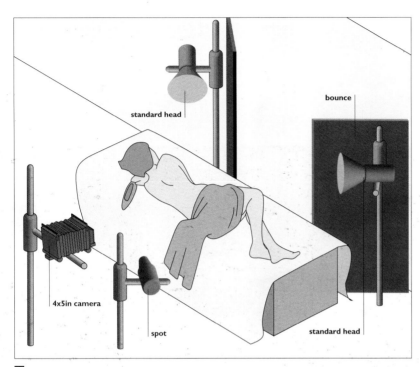

THERE ARE TWO ELEMENTS TO THE SUBJECT OF THE PHOTOGRAPH, AND A DIFFERENT LIGHTING APPROACH FOR EACH.

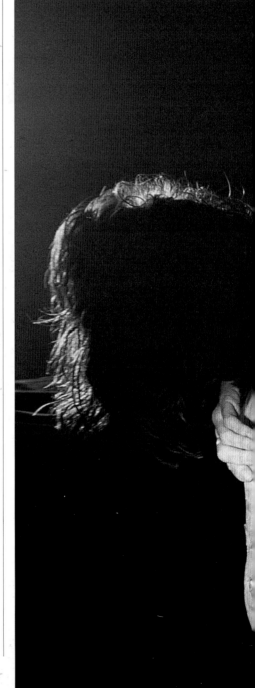

The model is lit by two daylight flash heads from behind and these, combined with the tungsten-balanced film, result in the blue tones that produce the illusion of moonlight streaming through a rear window. The two black flags control the light so that no unwanted light strays onto the black backdrop cloth.

Meanwhile, the shoe is lit by a focusing spot, which has been corrected by an 85 filter placed in front of the flash head, to balance it for the tungsten film stock. The shoe is therefore technically "correct" in terms of colour renditioning and sings out against the night-emulating areas of blue.

Photographer's comment:

This picture belongs to a series of "Dressed/Non-dressed" fashion accessories: that's why the shoe is held by the model in her hand behind her back.

► Although there are two heads at the rear, notice that one must dominate to give the effect of a moonlight source, while the other quietly fills without jeopardising the illusion

► It is possible to experiment with different combinations of film stock, lighting and filtration all in the same image, and a good formula can bring excellent results

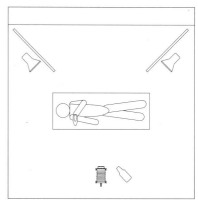

Plan View

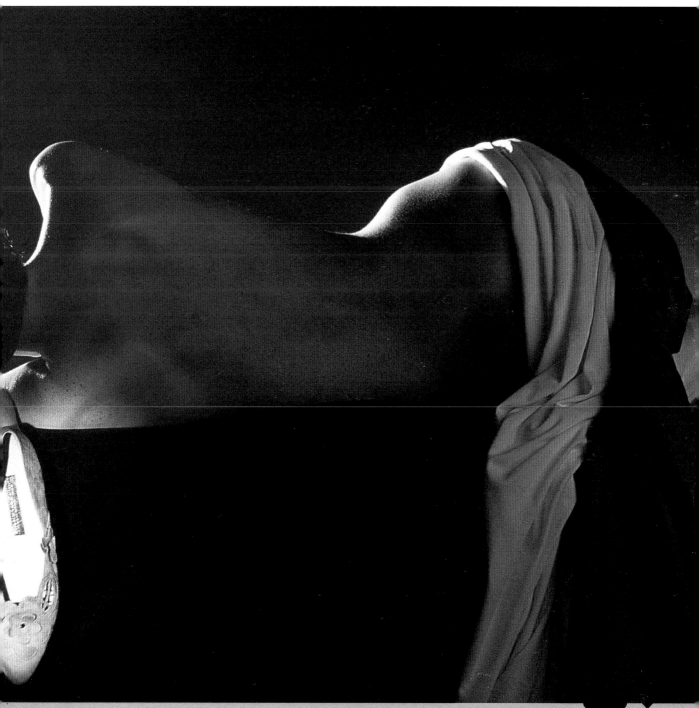

Photographer: **Guido Paternò Castello**

Client: **Ipiranga**

Use: **Calendar**

Assistant: **André Luís Moreado**

Art director: **Frederico Gelli**

Design: **Tatil Design**

Camera: **645**

Lens: **127mm**

Film: **EPP 100 pushed 1 stop**

Exposure: **6 seconds at f/16**

Lighting: **Available light**

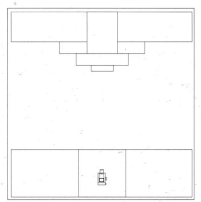

Plan View

U F O

▼

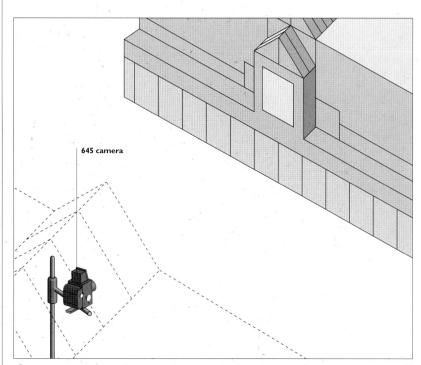

645 camera

Sᴏᴍᴇ ɪᴍᴀɢᴇs, ᴡʜɪʟᴇ ᴏʙᴠɪᴏᴜsʟʏ ᴘʜᴏᴛᴏɢʀᴀᴘʜs ᴏꜰ ʀᴇᴀʟ ᴛʜɪɴɢs, sᴇᴇᴍ ᴊᴜsᴛ ᴛᴏᴏ ᴘᴇʀꜰᴇᴄᴛ ᴛᴏ ʙᴇ ᴛʀᴜᴇ. Tʜᴀᴛ ᴍɪɢʜᴛ ᴡᴇʟʟ ʙᴇ ʙᴇᴄᴀᴜsᴇ ᴅɪɢɪᴛᴀʟ ᴍᴀɴɪᴘᴜʟᴀᴛɪᴏɴ ʜᴀs ʙᴇᴇɴ ᴜsᴇᴅ ᴛᴏ sᴍᴏᴏᴛʜ ᴏᴜᴛ ᴀɴʏ ʙʟᴇᴍɪsʜᴇs, ᴛᴏ ᴇᴠᴇɴ ᴏᴜᴛ ᴛʜᴇ ᴄᴏʟᴏᴜʀ ᴀɴᴅ, ᴘᴇʀʜᴀᴘs, ᴛᴏ ᴘʟᴀᴄᴇ ᴛʜᴇ ᴍᴏᴏɴ ᴏʙʟɪɢɪɴɢʟʏ ᴀᴛ ᴛʜᴇ ɪᴅᴇᴀʟ sɪᴢᴇ ɪɴ ᴛʜᴇ ʙᴇsᴛ ᴘᴏssɪʙʟᴇ ᴘᴏsɪᴛɪᴏɴ.

The requirement for light here was total ambient darkness (see Photographer's comment below). In other words, Guido Paternò Castello was waiting for a location setting to transform itself into typical studio conditions: smooth darkness containing a lit subject. It was very important to balance the exposure between seeing into the mini-market and seeing the space-age style canopy above the forecourt outside. In this case, any infelicities could, of course, always be taken care of later. The interior of the store is the most complicated and "busy" part of the image and is, therefore, the least flexible (manipulable) part so it makes sense to expose primarily for that area, keeping the digital technology as a back-up for the simpler architectural forms.

► *Don't manipulate just because you can, but only because you choose to. Sometimes less can be more, and a more restrained use of the software can result in a stark and striking image*

Photographer's comment:

I waited for total darkness (9 o'clock at night) to expose the film to the gas station roof and the convenience store. The image was later manipulated digitally to place the moon. The software was Photoshop 3.0 and the computer was a Power Mac 8100/80.

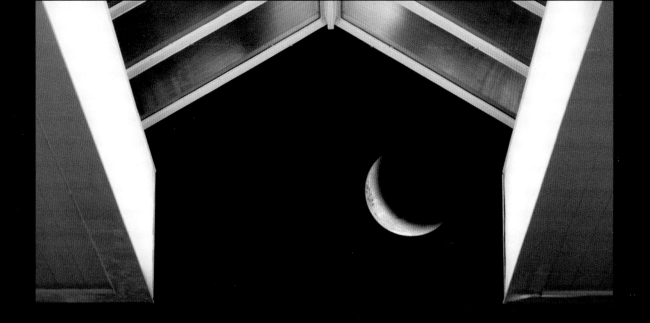

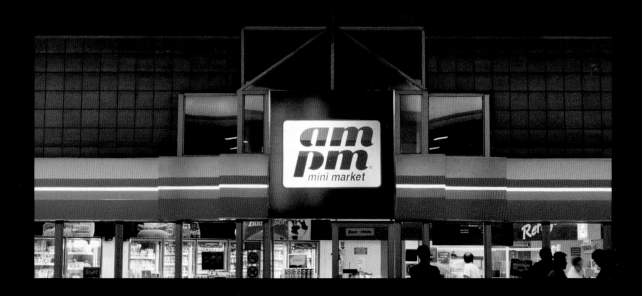

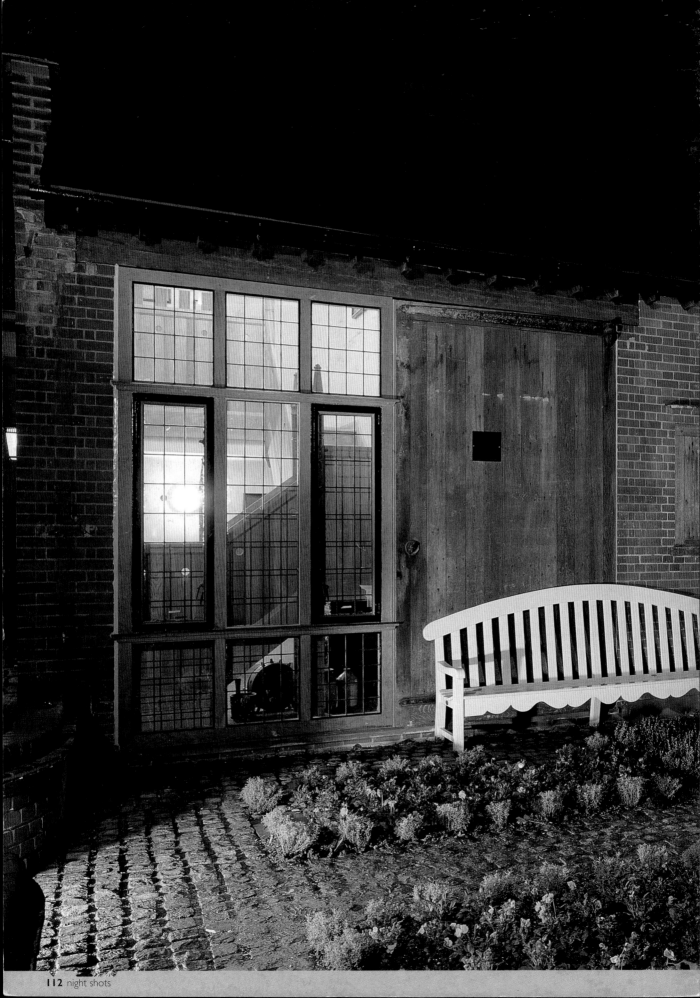

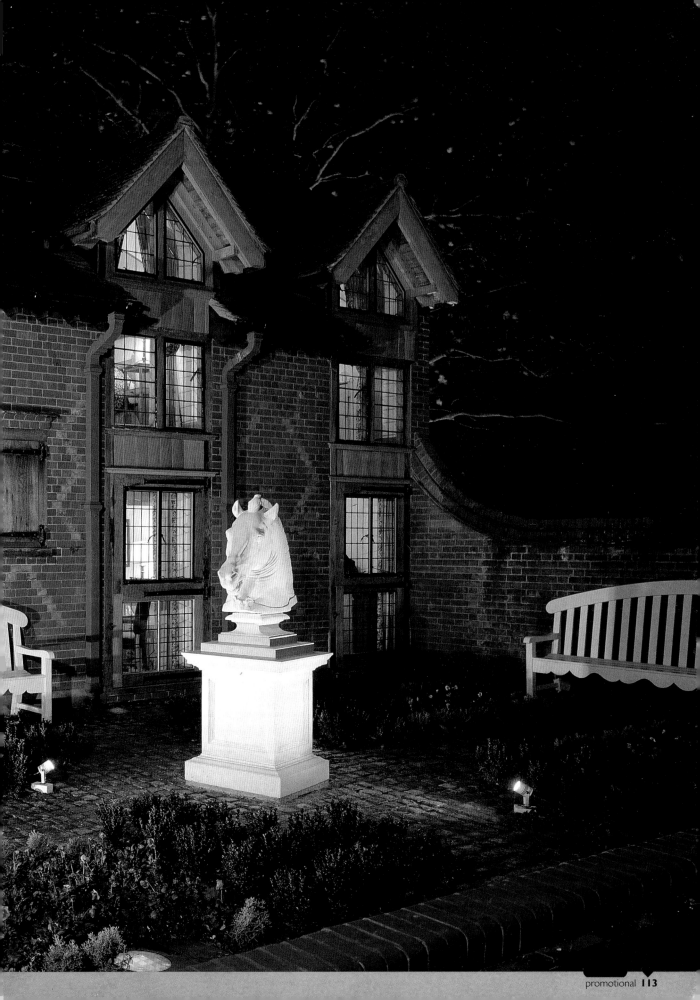

Photographer: **Harry Lomax**

Client: **Courage Ltd**

Use: **Editorial**

Art director: **Paragon Design**

Camera: **4x5 inch**

Lens: **65mm**

Film: **Fuji RDP**

Exposure: **2 seconds at f/16**

Lighting: **Flash and tungsten**

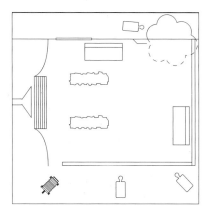

Plan View

L O D G E   E X T E R I O R

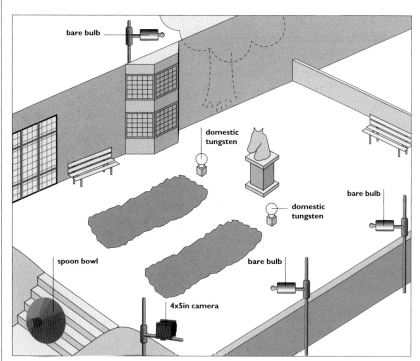

THIS SHOT LOOKS VERY NATURAL TO THE EYE, AND IT WILL COME AS NO SURPRISE TO LEARN THAT A GREAT DEAL OF THOUGHT AND EFFORT WAS PUT INTO MAKING IT APPEAR SO.

All the rooms in the Lodge are lit by flash as well as having the domestic tungsten lights switched on. The flash allows detail to be seen through the windows, while the tungsten lamps add warmth and ambience. It is these domestic lamps that dictate the need for a 2-second exposure; any less and the warmth would not register sufficiently.

The same applies to the horse sculpture. The front façade and courtyard garden are illuminated by flash but the two visible tungsten halogen spot lights also lend warmth to the sculpture.

Two bare-bulb mono-heads are positioned to the right of the camera, one giving definition to the near garden wall and to the central area of the house front, and the second one is directed at the far bench and the right side of the house. A mono-head bounced off a reflector sends further light into the courtyard along the path and steps just out of view on the left of frame.

Finally, a flash set about 5m high lights the visible upper branches of the tree to give texture and interest to the background.

Photographer's comment:

The brief was to show an attractive interior and exterior sitting area. It was taken in November (wet) so it was decided that it had to be a night shot.

► *Note that mono heads or Morris lamps are in most of the bedrooms of the Lodge as well as on the staircase on the right.*

Photographer: **Myk Semenytsh**

Use: **Corporate Christmas card for**

Drawing Board

Model: **Sophie McDonnell at Boss Agencies**

Manchester

Art director: **Tony Owen**

Camera: **RB67**

Lens: **180mm**

Film: **Fuji RDP**

Exposure: **1 second at f/16**

Lighting: **Tungsten and electronic flash**

Props and background: **Holly and apple**

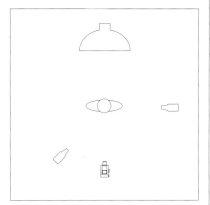

Plan View

▼

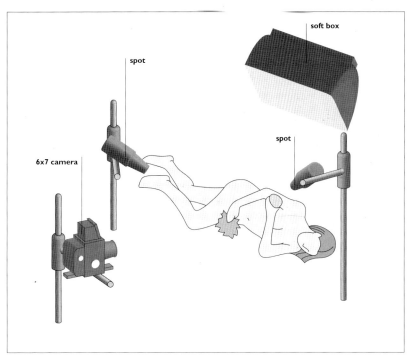

soft box

spot

spot

6x7 camera

THE PROPS USED ARE ESSENTIAL FOR THE PUN OF THE MESSAGE TO WORK. THE HOLLY REPRESENTS CHRISTMAS, THE APPLE REPRESENTS EVE, THE FIRST WOMAN AND THE ORIGINAL TEMPTRESS, AND THE TWO IDEAS JUXTAPOSED GIVE A NEW SLANT TO A VISUALISATION OF THE TERM "CHRISTMAS EVE." MYK SEMENYTSH EXPLAINS:

"This was shot for Drawing Board Design Consultants for use as a Christmas card. The card was sent out with just the message inside, 'Christmas Eve'. The only clue of identity is on the back, i.e. their telephone number, again a clever use of type. The card reads: 'Plus four four [zero], one six one, two three six, five five, ho ho' (+44 [0] 161 236 5500). The response was fantastic, with the agency being inundated with telephone calls."

The two vital points of interest in this shot, the holly and the apple, each have a tungsten spot light of their own. The model is stretched on her side with a haze light positioned above and behind to give a rim light along the outline of the body but not much detail in the foreground. This gives a landscape effect with the body forming an evening horizon, an extra layer of pun on the theme.

► *The logic of visual puns needs to be worked through carefully with the client when establishing the brief*

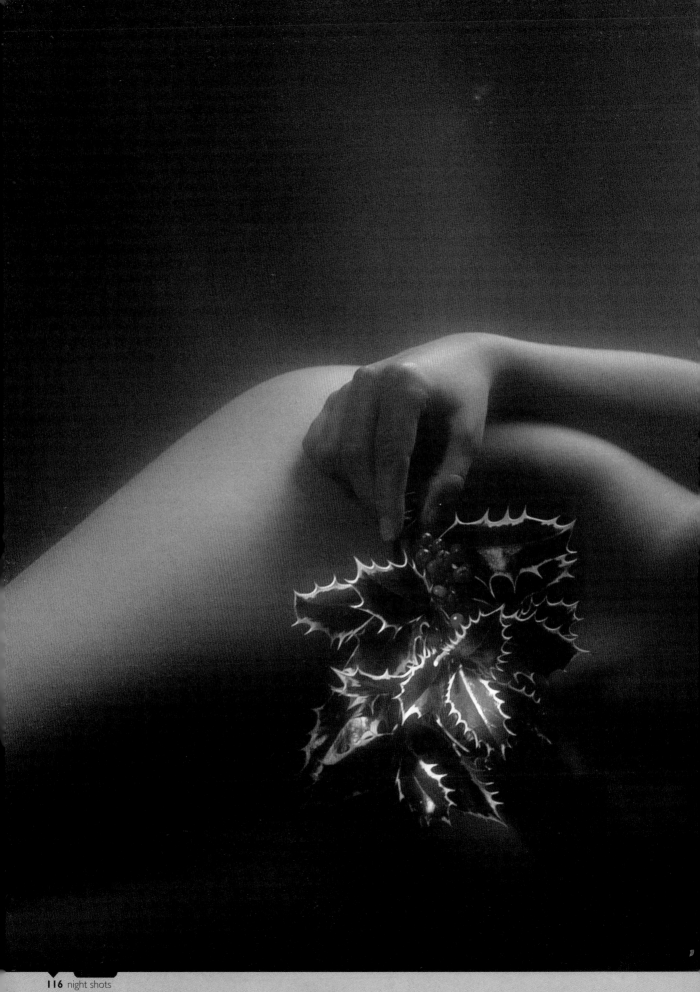

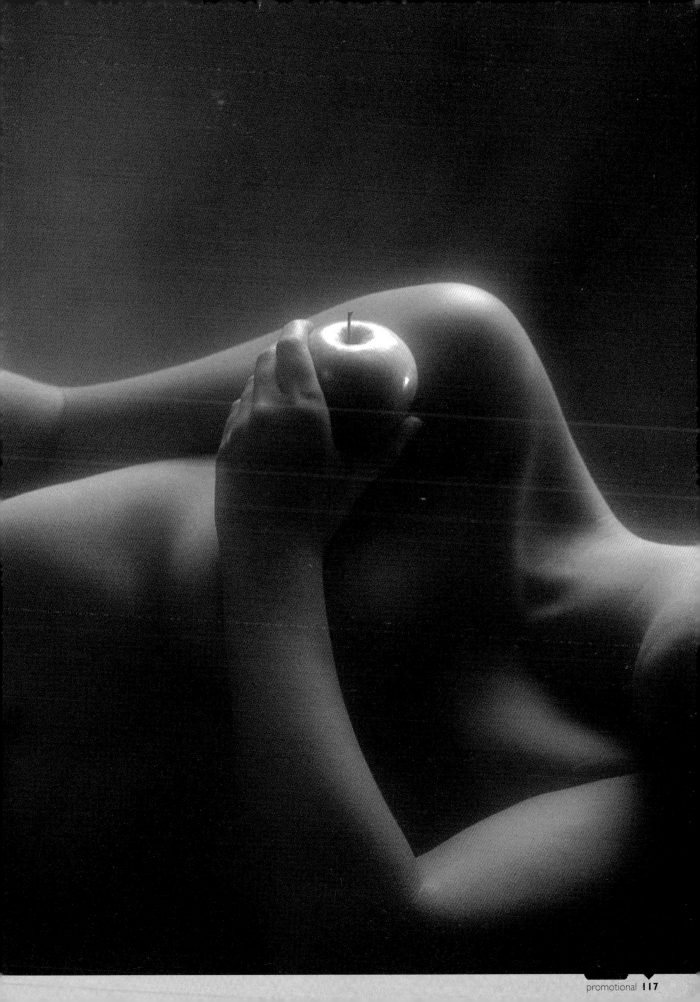

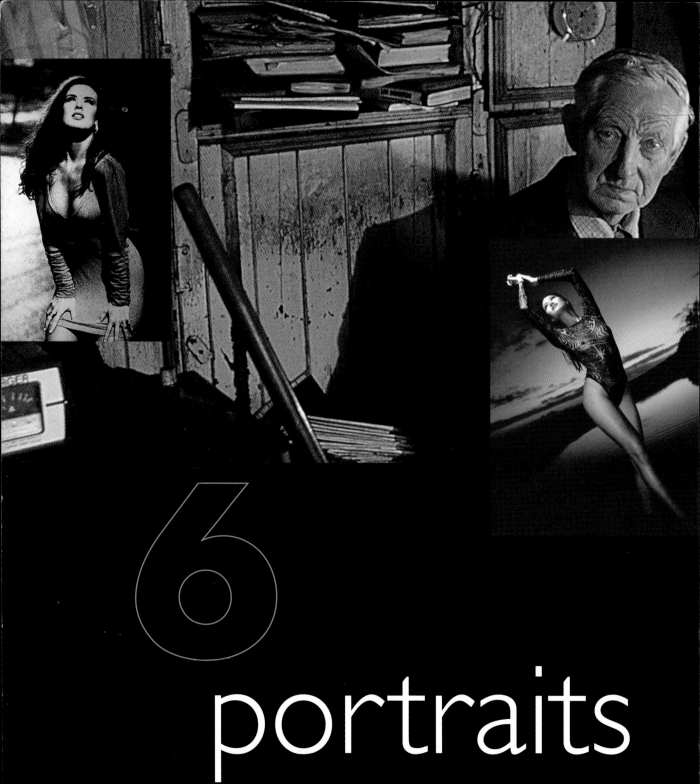

6
portraits

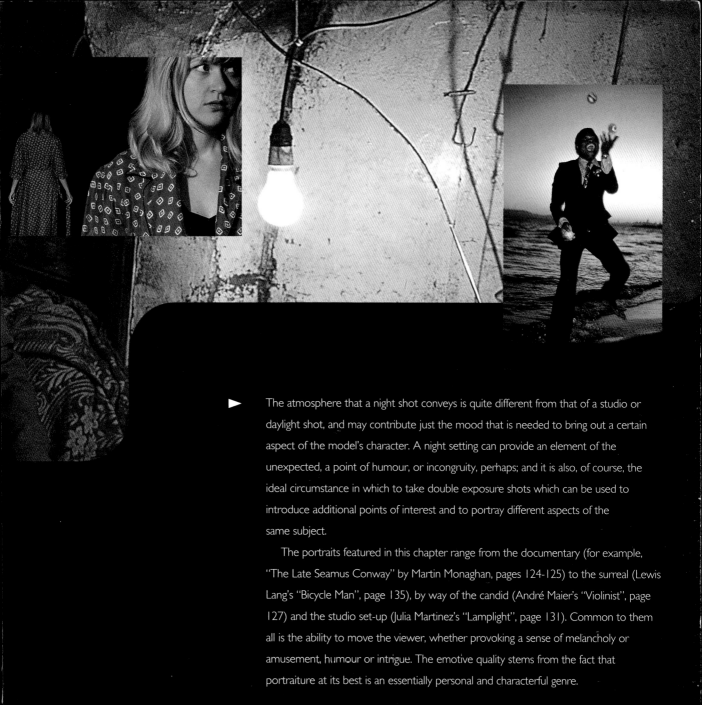

▶ The atmosphere that a night shot conveys is quite different from that of a studio or daylight shot, and may contribute just the mood that is needed to bring out a certain aspect of the model's character. A night setting can provide an element of the unexpected, a point of humour, or incongruity, perhaps; and it is also, of course, the ideal circumstance in which to take double exposure shots which can be used to introduce additional points of interest and to portray different aspects of the same subject.

The portraits featured in this chapter range from the documentary (for example, "The Late Seamus Conway" by Martin Monaghan, pages 124-125) to the surreal (Lewis Lang's "Bicycle Man", page 135), by way of the candid (André Maier's "Violinist", page 127) and the studio set-up (Julia Martinez's "Lamplight", page 131). Common to them all is the ability to move the viewer, whether provoking a sense of melancholy or amusement, humour or intrigue. The emotive quality stems from the fact that portraiture at its best is an essentially personal and characterful genre.

Photographer: **Lewis Lang**

Use: **Exhibition/print sales**

Model: **James Esoimeme**

Camera: **35mm**

Lens: **50mm f/2 Nikkor**

Film: **Kodachrome 25**

Exposure: **1/60 second, wide open**

Lighting: **Available light, on-camera flash**

Props and background: **3 juggling balls, beach in Alaneda, California**

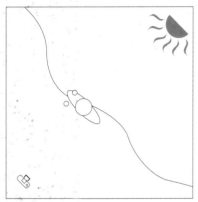

Plan View

JAMES JUGGLING IN THE WAVES

▼

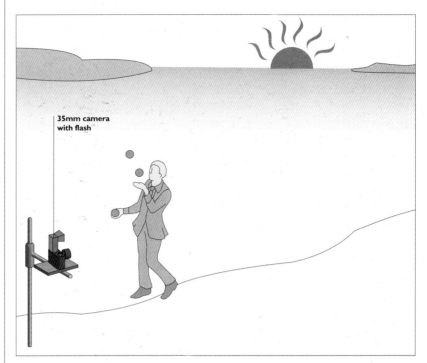

35mm camera
with flash

Tнis рнотоgraph was taken at or near the flash sync speed of Lewis Lang's Nikon F3 in order to freeze the action of the juggling balls in mid-air, without the "ghosting" that would have been a problem with longer shutter speeds, given the significant level of ambient light.

On-camera flash filled in the subject in what otherwise would have been a silhouette of James and the balls. Lewis comments that, "We would have missed out on his wonderful facial expression and, pardon the pun, his fish-out-of-water yet appropriate stylish formal suit that he wears!" The beach, water and sky become the perfect background for this outdoor but highly controlled "studio-esque" shot, providing balance as well as colour. The clear sky, with smoothly graduated tones, has no busy clouds to distract from the most important part of the foreground while the area of gently rippling sea adds texture and interest to the lower portion of the image.

► *Pressing the shutter at the right moment requires good hand-eye coordination and reflexes*

Photographer's comment:

On-camera flash has a harsh flat, shadowless lighting that emphasises shape that I happen to like, but some people don't. Here it works well, I think.

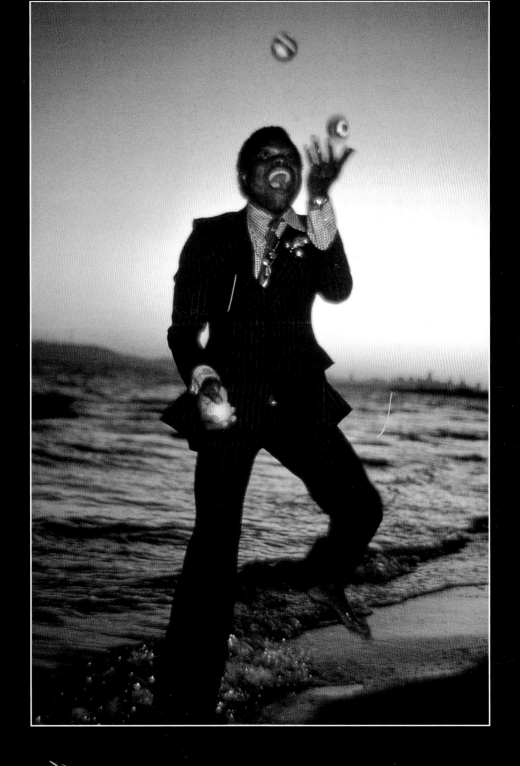

Photographer: **Tim Orden**

Client: **Personal work**

Use: **Stock**

Model: **Celeste**

Assistant: **Donna Orden**

Make-up: **Donna Orden**

Camera: **35mm**

Lens: **28mm**

Film: **Realla**

Exposure: **1/2 second at f/4**

Lighting: **Available light plus electronic flash, 2 heads**

Props and background: **Pool at bird sanctuary, Maalaea, Hawaii**

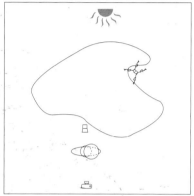

Plan View

CELESTE AND THE CELESTIAL BODY

▼

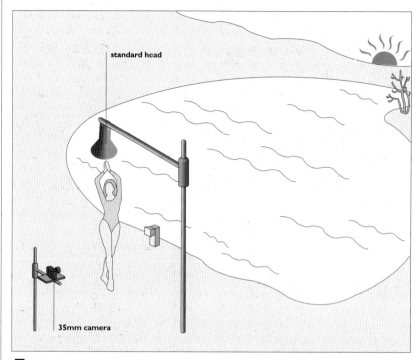

standard head

35mm camera

TIM ORDEN USED A LOCATION THAT HE KNEW OF AT A BIRD SANCTUARY, WITH A SHALLOW POND. TIM KNEW THAT THE SKY AND WATER WOULD REFLECT FROM THIS VERY SHALLOW POND AS THE SUN WENT DOWN.

To enhance the dreamy quality of the composition he placed a remotely triggered coloured flash about 7m behind the model, on the ground. This gives a warm rim light and glowing back lighting to the subject.

The main light was held in position on a boom, directly over the model's head to give what Tim likes to call "The Spielberg Effect". In other words, the light floods down from directly above while the model gazes heavenwards, at something glorious just out of our view. Not only is the angle of the face and the light falling upon it flattering to the model, but it also imparts the feeling that there is a "celestial body" of some kind above her.

Photographer's comment:

Celeste is a wonderful Hawaiian girl who can be very graceful. I have photographed her many times and every time is a joy. A typical Hawaiian beauty, "C", as I call her, speaks softly and listens intently. She has an inner power that commands your respect.

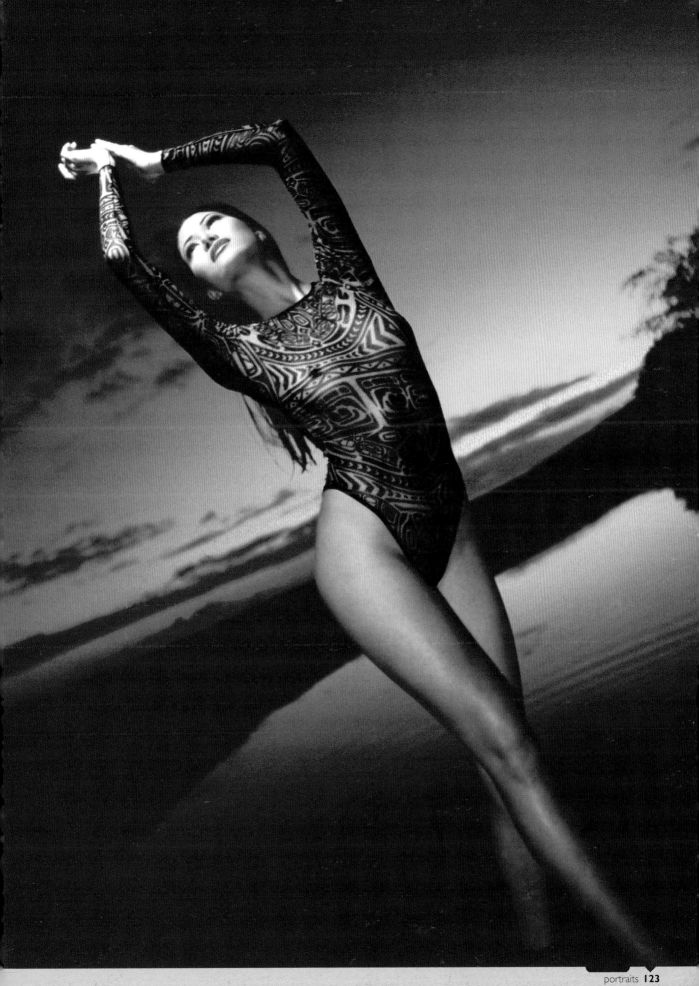

THE LATE SEAMUS CONWAY

Photographer: **Martin Monaghan**
Camera: **Nikon F4**
Lens: **24mm**
Film: **Fuji Velvia**
Exposure: **1/60 second at f/2**

▼

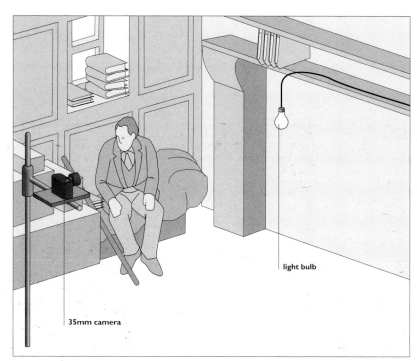

light bulb

35mm camera

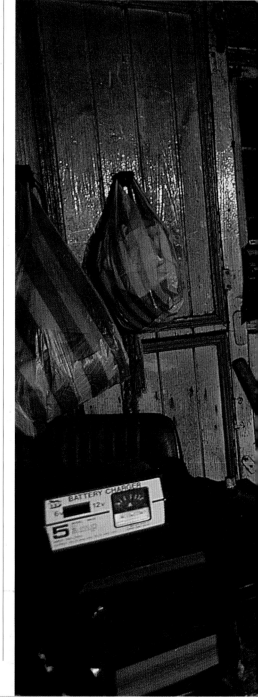

THIS TOUCHING AND AFFECTIONATE PORTRAIT OF AN ELDERLY MAN IN HIS OWN HOME IS AS MUCH DOCUMENTARY AS IT IS PORTRAITURE. THE FASCINATING DETAIL OF THE INTERIOR PROVIDES MASSES OF INTEREST WHILE THE EXPRESSION OF THE SUBJECT ENGAGES AND DRAWS THE VIEWER IN. IT COMES AS NO SURPRISE TO LEARN THAT THE SHOT WAS TAKEN AS PART OF A DOCUMENTARY SERIES, RECORDING THE LIVES OF RURAL ELDERLY PEOPLE.

The extreme warmth of the shot comes from a tungsten household bulb in conjunction with the daylight-balanced film used, providing the orange glow that gives the impression and cosy mood of firelight. This bulb is the main source, and is obviously a point source, but it is also reflected by the wall behind it.

The light from the domestic bulb is supplemented by the use of very low power fill-in flash, well judged so as to allow the viewer to see into the shadow detail without destroying the overall atmosphere and ambience.

Photographer's comment:

This image is from a series documenting the rural elderly whose lifestyle may soon be lost forever.

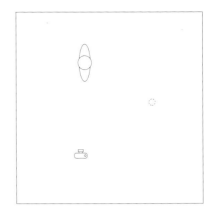

Plan View

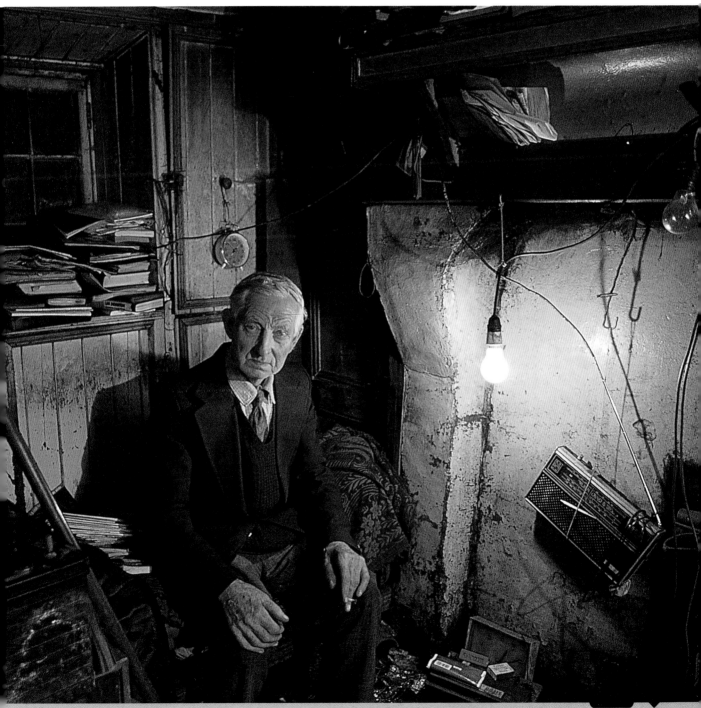

Photographer: **André Maier**

Use: **Stock**

Camera: **35mm**

Lens: **100mm macro**

Film: **Fujichrome 1600 ASA**

Exposure: **1/30 second at f/2.8**

Lighting: **Available light**

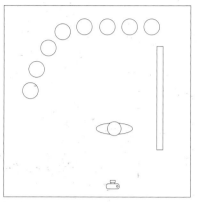

Plan View

VIOLINIST

▼

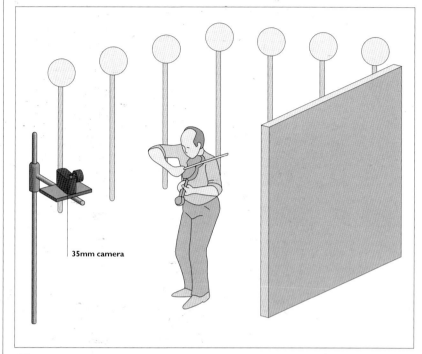

35mm camera

THIS CANDID PORTRAIT OF A BUSKER PLAYING THE VIOLIN WAS TAKEN NEAR THE NATIONAL FILM THEATRE, LONDON. THE VIOLINIST WAS PERFORMING UNDER WATERLOO BRIDGE, WITH THE STREET LIGHTS ALONG THE EMBANKMENT BEHIND HIM AND THE ILLUMINATION UNDER THE BRIDGE PROVIDING THE NEARER SOURCE.

The row of lights in the background provides a halo of brilliance behind the head while the red lighting on the underside of the bridge structure illuminates the violinist's head and hand.

The violin body has some fill light falling on it, and reflected in it from a white wall next to the subject. Notice, too, the bright streak of light picked out along the length of the bow hairs. The relatively slow exposure gives the blur of the hand and shows the motion of the violinist.

Photographer's comment:

The red light is from regular street lamps.

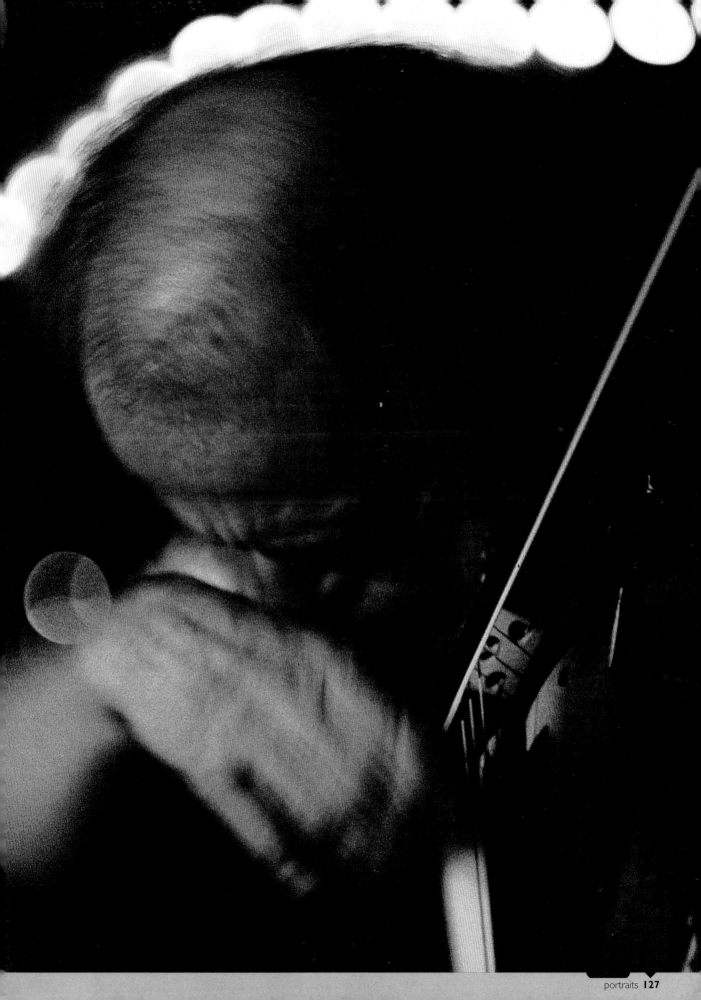

Photographers: **Ben Lagunas and Alex Kuri**

Client: *Vogue*

Use: **Editorial**

Model: **Sandy Possety**

Assistants: **Natasha, Victoria and Suzanne**

Art director: **Nóe Aqudo**

Stylist: **Felix/Charle**

Camera: **Hasselblad 205TCC**

Lens: **180 cf Sonnar**

Film: **Kodak Tmax**

Exposure: **1/30 second at f/5.6**

Lighting: **Available light**

Location: **Street**

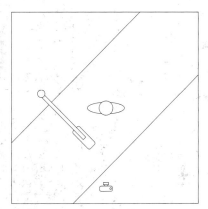

Plan View

N I G H T   F A S H I O N   I I

▼

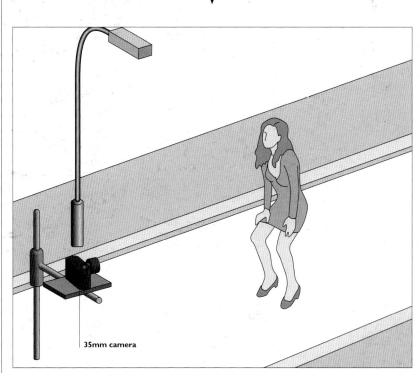

35mm camera

THE MODEL IN THIS DECEPTIVELY SIMPLE LOOKING SET-UP HAS BEEN EXPERTLY POSITIONED TO GET THE VERY BEST OUT OF THE SETTING AND LIGHT AVAILABLE. THE SLIGHTLY HIGH ANGLE OF THE CAMERA KEEPS THE ROAD SURFACE IN VIEW ON THE LEFT TO CONTRAST WITH THE MODEL'S CLOTHING, SEPARATING HER FROM THE BACKGROUND. EQUALLY IMPORTANT IS THE SEPARATION BETWEEN HER AND THE LACK OF LIGHT TO THE RIGHT: THE POINT TO NOTE HERE IS THAT EFFECTIVE CONTRAST OF TONE CAN WORK WITH LIGHT AGAINST DARK, DARK AGAINST LIGHT, RELATIVELY DARK AGAINST EVEN DARKER … AND SO ON.

► *With black and white film, remember that you are working with tonal range rather than colour to achieve separation. Contrast can be thought of as relative points on a gradient, rather than absolute positions at the extremes*

The choice of equipment and good direction of the model also play a major part. The long lens throws the background out of focus. The model is positioned below and to the side of the street light and has been well instructed to tilt the head upwards to catch the full light on the face. Notice the wonderful rim light on the hair, with just enough light to achieve separation between the model and the area behind, giving an almost three-dimensional sense of recession between foreground and background. The costume is well selected, with the ruffles providing excellent texture for the light to play upon, while the earring provides a reflective surface to catch a highlight. The fact that the light is almost directly overhead means that deep shadow occurs under all lower surfaces; for example, below the hands, skirt line and throat, again heightening the three-dimensional impression.

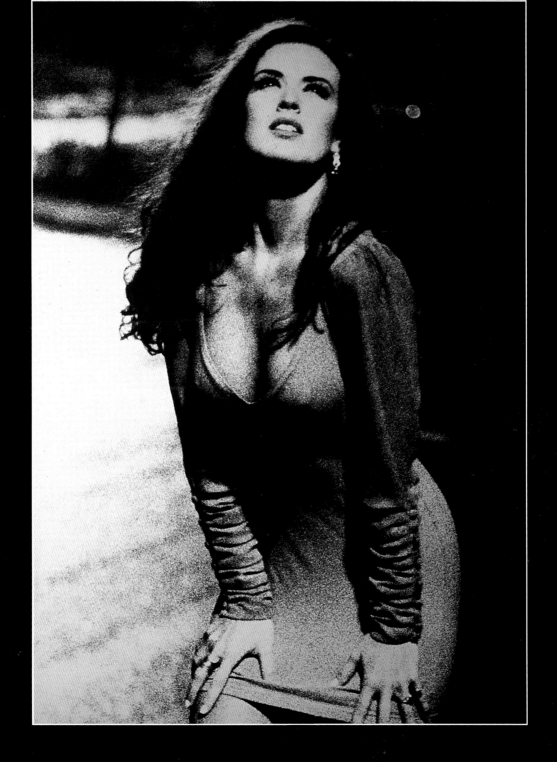

Photographer: **Julia Martinez**

Use: **Portfolio work**

Camera: **Mamiya 645**

Lens: **300mm**

Film: **Kodak 100**

Exposure: **f/11**

Lighting: **Lamp**

Props: **Smoke machine**

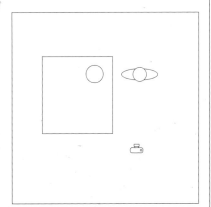

Plan View

L A M P   L I G H T

▼

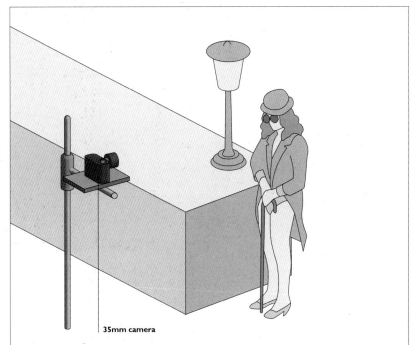

35mm camera

THIS SIMPLE STUDIO SET-UP EMULATES A NIGHT-TIME STREET SCENE TO GOOD EFFECT, EVOKING IMAGES OF CHARLIE CHAPLIN IN HIS DISTINCTIVE BOWLER HAT, OR, PERHAPS, JUDY GARLAND AS ONE OF A PAIR OF DOWN-AT-HEEL "COUPLE OF SWELLS", COMPLETE WITH UMBRELLA AND SUIT. THE DRAMATIC CONNOTATIONS ARE OBVIOUS, AND ARE CREATED BY THE THEATRICAL LIGHTING AND MOODY STYLING.

The only lighting is from the street lamp above and to the side of the model. Precise positioning of the model in relation to the light and careful direction of such details as the tilt of the head and angle of the hat result in a bold shaft of light across part of the face while the other side remains in deep shade.

The chiaroscuro *film-noir* look is bold and striking and plays up the graphic elements of the composition to good effect.

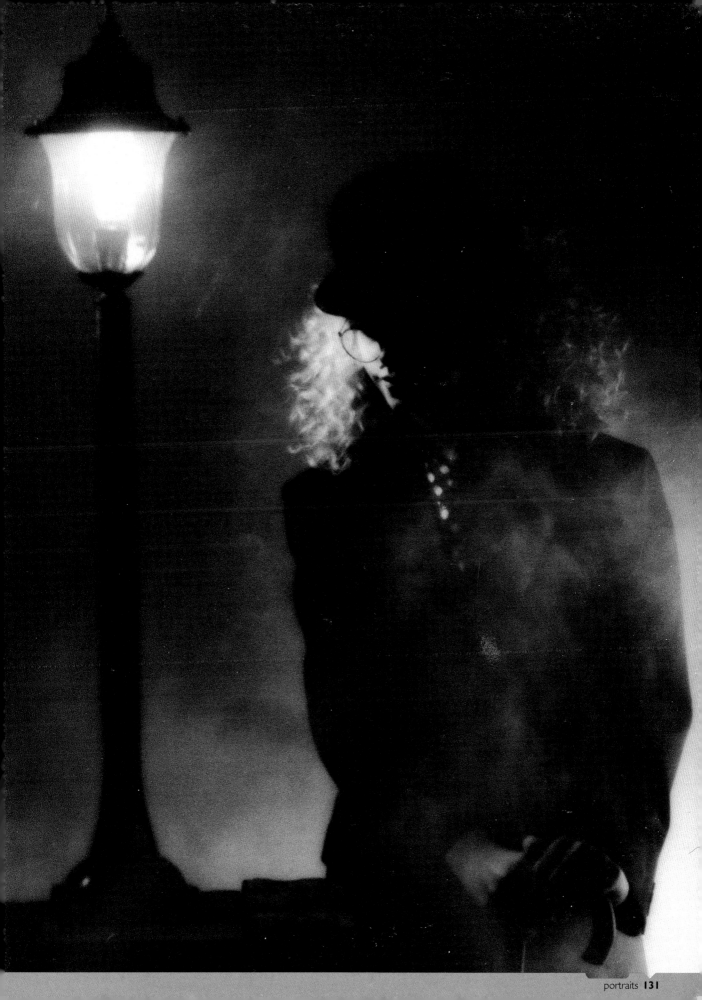

A M A N D A

▼

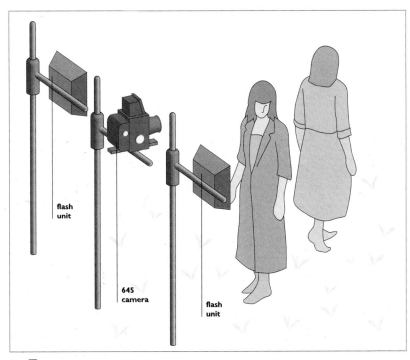

Photographer: **Emma Frater**

Use: **Portfolio**

Assistant: **Matthew Frater**

Model: **Amanda Barnes**

Camera: **645**

Lens: **150mm**

Film: **Fuji Velvia**

Exposure: **Double exposure, f/5.6**

Lighting: **On-camera flash**

Props and background: **A field at night. Model wearing 1940s satin dressing gown.**

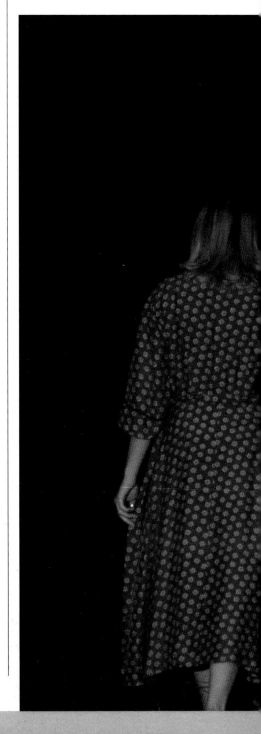

Eᴍᴍᴀ Fʀᴀᴛᴇʀ ᴄʜᴏsᴇ ᴀ ꜰɪᴇʟᴅ ᴏɴ ᴀ ᴅᴀʀᴋ ɴɪɢʜᴛ ᴀs ᴛʜᴇ ʟᴏᴄᴀᴛɪᴏɴ ꜰᴏʀ ᴛʜɪs ᴅᴏᴜʙʟᴇ ᴇxᴘᴏsᴜʀᴇ sʜᴏᴛ. "A ᴅᴀʀᴋ ʙᴀᴄᴋɢʀᴏᴜɴᴅ ɪs ᴇssᴇɴᴛɪᴀʟ ɪꜰ ʏᴏᴜ ᴡᴀɴᴛ ᴛᴏ ᴀᴠᴏɪᴅ ᴀ ɢʜᴏsᴛ-ʟɪᴋᴇ ɪᴍᴀɢᴇ," sʜᴇ ᴇxᴘʟᴀɪɴs.

For the first exposure, the model was relatively close to the camera and firmly in the right of the frame. The flash was hand-held to camera right, but still to the left of the model, giving side-lighting on the face.

Both the model and the assistant holding the flash were then re-positioned for the second shot, with the model now some distance away from the camera and this time in place in the left of frame. The flash was also moved, over to the left in order to retain a similar position in relation to the model as was used for the first exposure.

An exposure of f/5.6 was used for both shots.

Photographer's comment:

Usually I don't like to see the whites of the eyes; I prefer direct eye contact, but the model looking away helped with the idea of her walking away from herself.

► There was no need to halve the
exposure in this case because the
background was dark and the subject
was exposed on a confined area of the
film only once

► Consistency of lighting position is
standard practice for a double
exposure, but this does not necessarily
mean that the source has to remain in
one place. If the subject moves, the light
source needs to move in relation to the
subject to obtain a similar effect for the
second exposure

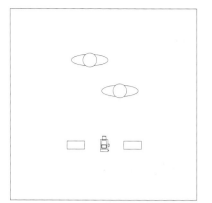

Plan View

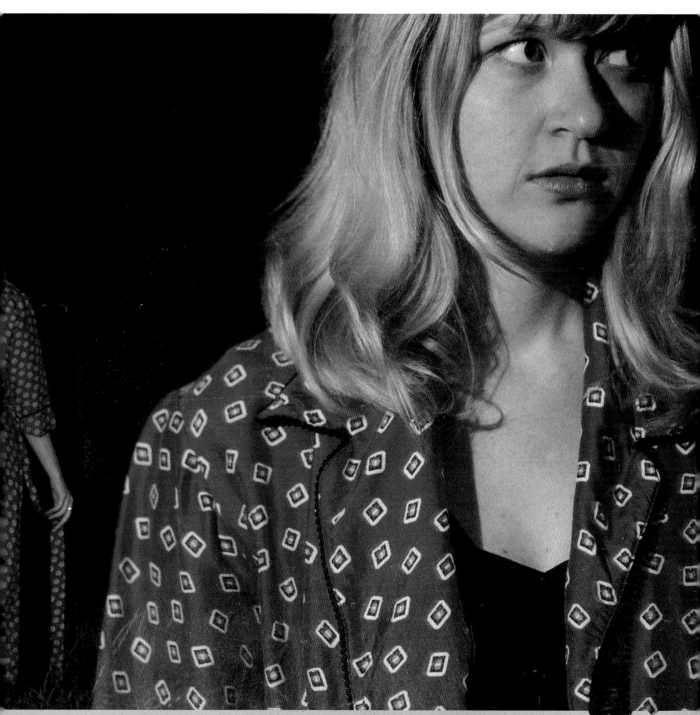

Photographer: **Lewis Lang**

Use: **Personal/print sales**

Camera: **35mm**

Lens: **50mm**

Film: **Kodachrome 64**

Exposure: **8 seconds**

Lighting: **Tungsten spotlights in window display**

Props and background: **Abstract sculpture of bicycle/man in a store's window display in Burlington, Ontario, Canada**

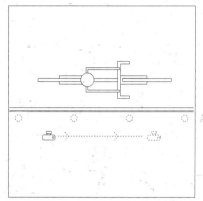

Plan View

BICYCLE MAN

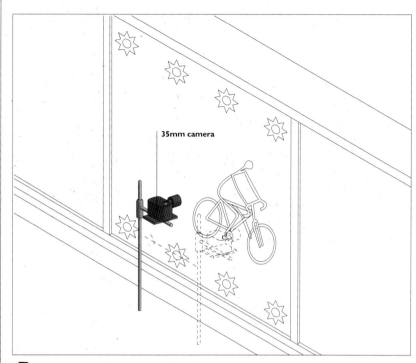

35mm camera

This is a classic example of opportunistic, spontaneous photography. Something unusual caught Lewis Lang's eye; he spotted the potential and drew on his imagination, skill and experience to pull off this fascinating shot. Lewis explains how it happened.

"I was literally window-shopping with my Pentax, just taking a walk to see what I could see (and photograph) when I spotted a small metallic-looking abstract sculpture of a man on a bicycle that seemed to be perpetually moving by its own power (no motors, batteries or electric cords). Though the bike man was pedalling in place, I decided to give the sculpture motion by panning my camera to the right (along the surface of the window to enhance my steadiness and avoid window reflections) so that the bicycle man would appear to be travelling to the right with his own repeated ghost image/blur trailing off behind to the left. I kept the camera static for the first 2–4 seconds (to register the bicycle man's sharp leading image on the right), then panned for the rest of the exposure's blurred trailing motion. Though I haven't been back to the location, it wouldn't surprise me to see the bicycle man still pedalling!"

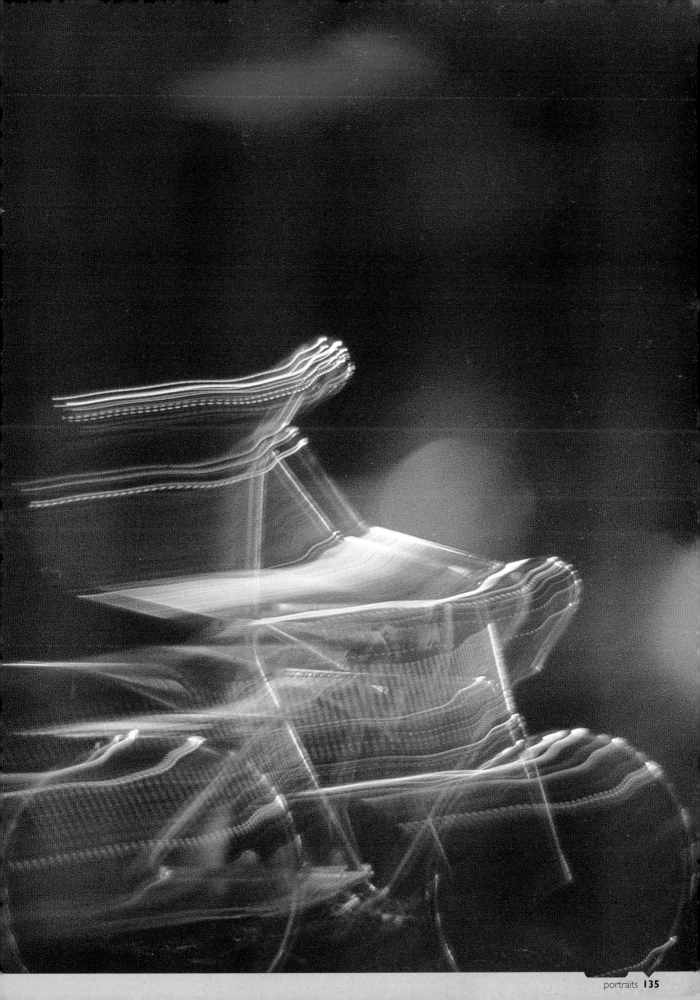

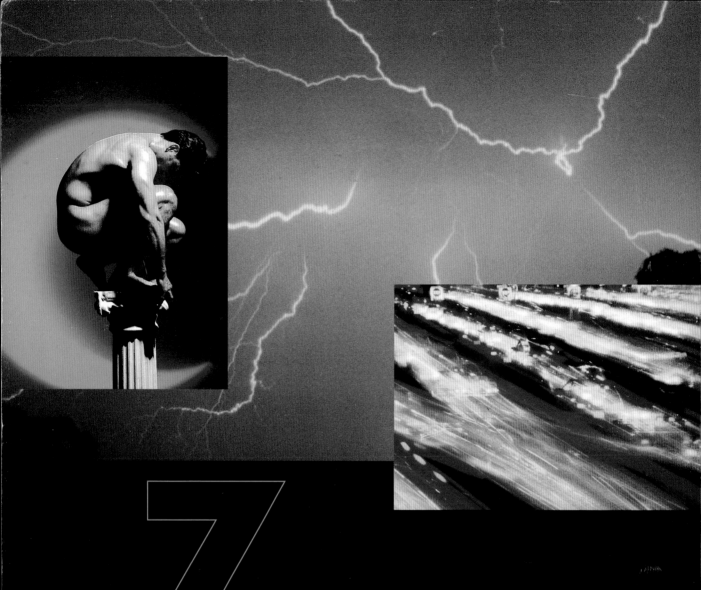

7

good night

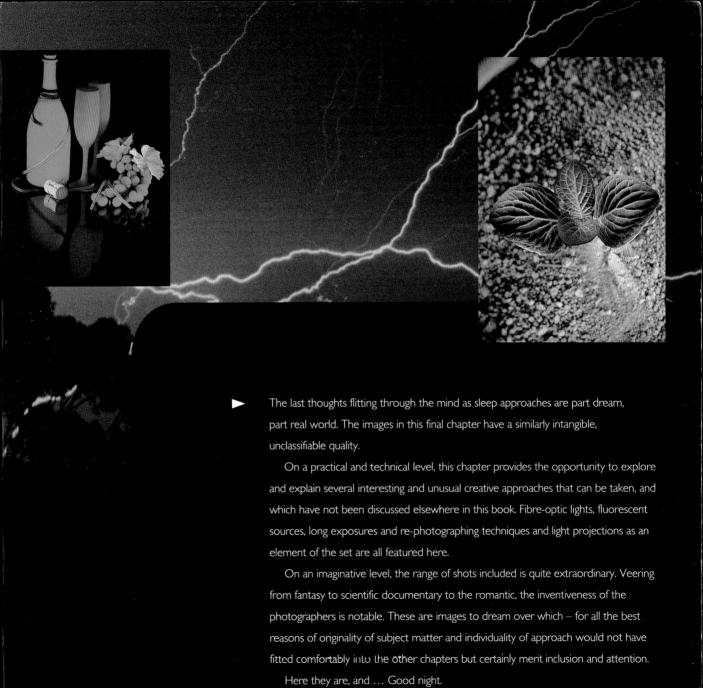

The last thoughts flitting through the mind as sleep approaches are part dream, part real world. The images in this final chapter have a similarly intangible, unclassifiable quality.

On a practical and technical level, this chapter provides the opportunity to explore and explain several interesting and unusual creative approaches that can be taken, and which have not been discussed elsewhere in this book. Fibre-optic lights, fluorescent sources, long exposures and re-photographing techniques and light projections as an element of the set are all featured here.

On an imaginative level, the range of shots included is quite extraordinary. Veering from fantasy to scientific documentary to the romantic, the inventiveness of the photographers is notable. These are images to dream over which – for all the best reasons of originality of subject matter and individuality of approach would not have fitted comfortably into the other chapters but certainly merit inclusion and attention.

Here they are, and … Good night.

PUKA-HUNTING

▼

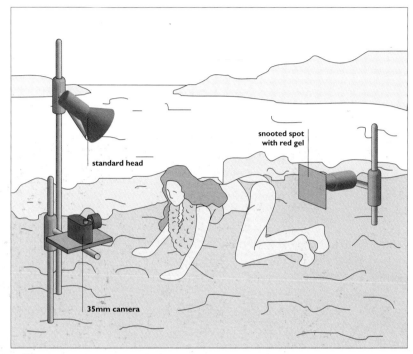

Photographer: **Tim Orden**

Client: **Personal work**

Use: **Stock**

Model: **Linda Uray**

Camera: **35mm**

Lens: **85mm**

Film: **Kodak Ektachrome 100**

Exposure: **Not recorded**

Lighting: **Available light plus electronic flash**

Props and background: **Beach**

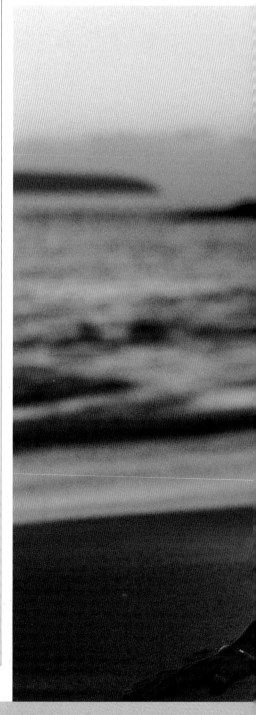

Tim Orden waited for the sun to be well below the horizon for this evening shot. "I am often challenged to have the patience to wait until the sky is right," he says. "For the most part it's not time until it's very dark and I have to use shutter speeds of 1/30 second."

A kicker red light was positioned behind the model to give the warm rim light (for example along the upper edge of the model's back arm) and to add colour and warmth to the sand texture in the background. A light on a boom gives a large pool of light from the front and above, providing clear light on the model's face and the upper sides of the body and limbs, while the lower legs and backs of the thighs remain in shadow, as do the right forearm and hand and areas of the hair. The result is a dramatic "in the spotlight" look which brings out the wealth of tones and textures in the various parts of the subject: the sand, the hair, the skin and the garland of flowers.

Photographer's comment:

I entitled this piece "Puka-hunting" because it's a ridiculous title. Imagine strolling along the beach and seeing this beautiful local girl searching for shells with "pukas" (holes) in them. I don't think so!

► Plan ahead for the practicalities of
shooting on location in the dark. Carry
torches and keep a good mental or
written inventory of all the equipment to
be rounded up at the end of the shoot

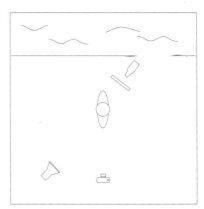

Plan View

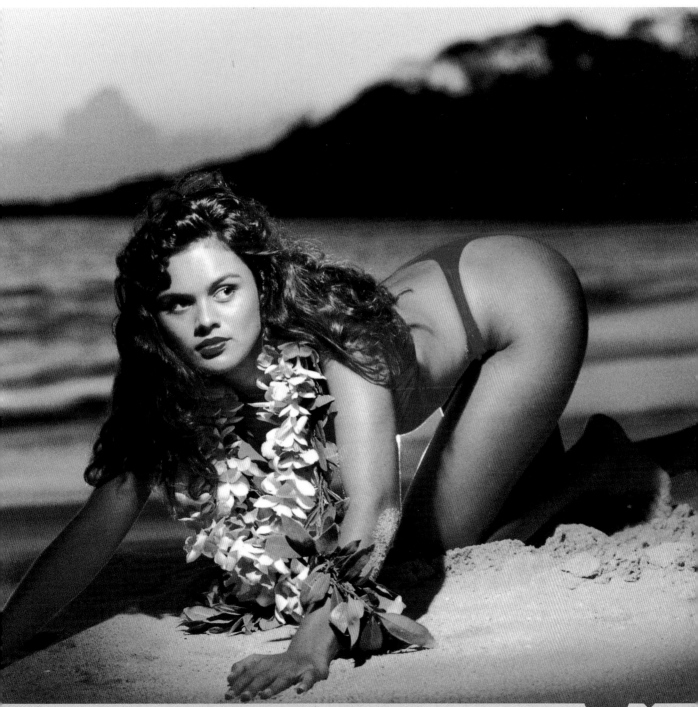

RUSH HOUR (DETAIL)

▼

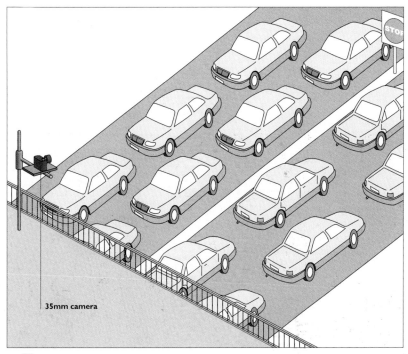

35mm camera

Photographer: **Lewis Lang**

Use: **Exhibition/print sales**

Camera: **35mm**

Lens: **25–50mm zoom (about 25mm)**

Film: **Kodachrome**

Exposure: **Long exposure**

Lighting: **Car headlights, street lamps**

Props and background: **Overpass, Fort Lee, New Jersey**

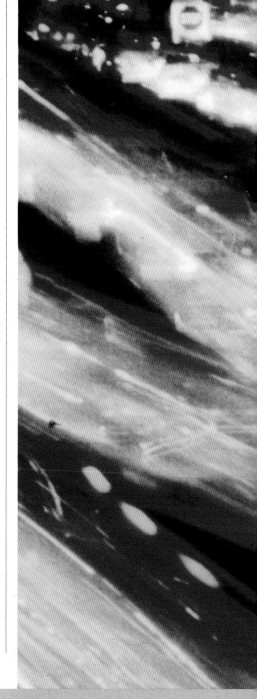

THIS SHOT IS ACTUALLY A "RE-PHOTOGRAPH" RATHER THAN A PHOTOGRAPH. HAVING INITIALLY TAKEN A WIDE-ANGLE SHOT ON A TRIPOD, LEWIS LANG THEN WANTED TO CLOSE IN ON JUST A SMALL AREA OF THE IMAGE. HE PROJECTED THE IMAGE AND RE-PHOTOGRAPHED JUST THE DETAIL THAT HE WANTED, A VERY SMALL AREA OF THE ORIGINAL FRAME. (NOTICE THE TEXTURE HERE WHICH IS ATTRIBUTABLE TO THE SURFACE WHERE THE IMAGE WAS PROJECTED.)

What we see here is the final image on Cibachrome (Ilford De Luxe), used, as Lewis puts it, "to pop the reds to blood red: anybody in New Jersey knows that rush hour is murder!"

Lewis took numerous versions of this shot, experimenting with long exposures lasting for anything from several seconds to several minutes. Some cars were moving at speed while others were slower or stationary. This gives an impression of frenetic car streaks as well as ghostly impressions of static cars. The use of a small aperture ensures a comparatively high level of detail for a shot of this kind.

Photographer's comment:

There is now a fence along the railings of the overpass where I took this picture. Moral: shoot your shot now! There may not be a second chance!

► *Don't assume your location will never change, or that you can always go back and do another session*

► *Printing techniques can contribute to the final colour just as much as the lighting*

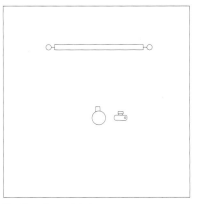

Plan View of second shot

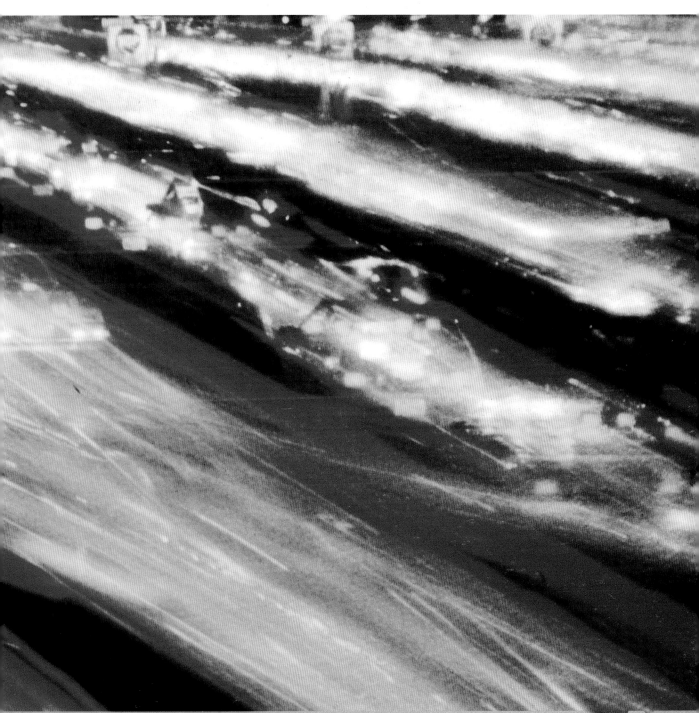

Photographer: **Bauer**

Client: **Bauer Cards**

Use: **Cards**

Model: **Alexandre Houck**

Assistant: **Kleber de Aravjo**

Camera: **35mm**

Lens: **200mm**

Film: **Fuji RDP developed in C41 process**

Exposure: **f/8**

Lighting: **Electronic flash, 3 heads**

Props and background: **Blue-painted background, rope and steps for security**

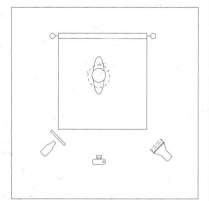

Plan View

B I R D M A N

▼

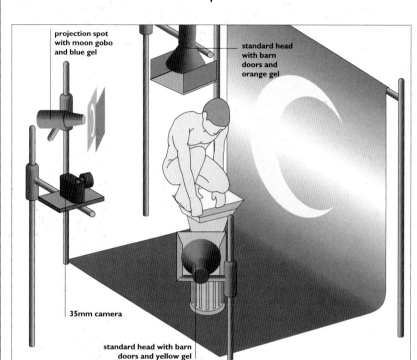

projection spot with moon gobo and blue gel

standard head with barn doors and orange gel

35mm camera

standard head with barn doors and yellow gel

THREE LIGHTS ARE INVOLVED IN THIS SHOT, BUT ONLY TWO OF THEM ARE ILLUMINATING THE SUBJECT. THE THIRD IS A PROJECTION SPOT THAT PROVIDES PART OF THE SUBJECT ITSELF, DISPLAYING THE CRESCENT MOON MOTIF ON THE BACKDROP.

The projection spot could have been focused sharply to give a crisp edge to the moon but here a softer outline is in keeping with the dream-like ambience. There are two standard heads, one high on the left lighting the back, the other low on the right lighting the lower part of the column. The height and direction of the upper head gives good graduation along the curvature of the back to echo the shape of the moon. The directionality of these lights is controlled by large snoots and barn doors to avoid interference with the moon-creating spot, both in terms of crossed beams of light and falling light on the backdrop.

The standard heads are both used in conjunction with coloured gels (orange and yellow respectively) giving a golden tone to the subject.

► *Crossed beams of coloured light may have an effect on the resulting colour depending on relative intensities*

Photographer's comment:

The background light (moon) is 1 stop brighter than the model's light (model's light: f/8, background light: f/11).

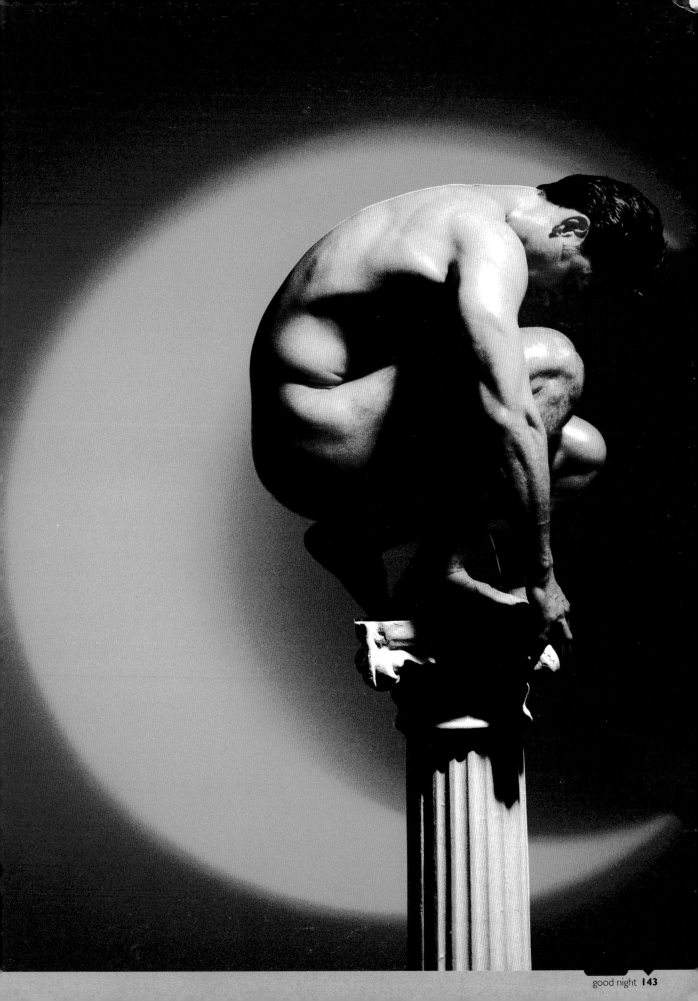

Photographer: **Tan Wee Khiang**

Client: **Design Objectives**

Use: **Presentation proposal**

Camera: **4x5 inch**

Lens: **150mm at f/5.6**

Film: **Agfa RS ISO 100**

Exposure: **2 minutes at f/16**

Lighting: **Tungsten (fibre optic)**

Props and background: **Seedling in a pot in a garden**

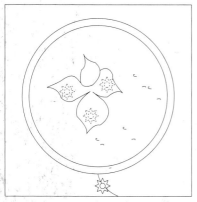

Plan View

▼

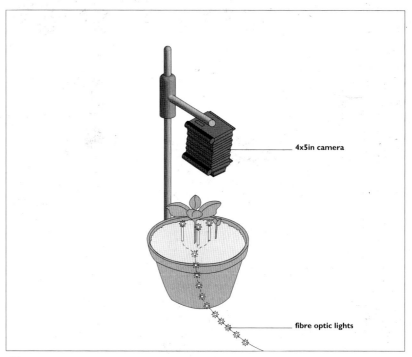

4x5in camera

fibre optic lights

Fibre optics facilitate controllable, directional, close-in lighting for small-scale subjects. This tiny seedling (shown at approximately life size below) was lit from beneath using a separate optic for each individual leaf. Even the soil in the pot has been lit separately from a very low angle.

The leaves are partially translucent and seem to glow from within. The close-up, individual lighting for each separate leaf effectively brings out the texture of the veins and structure in fascinating detail.

Notice the time of the exposure; a fairly lengthy 2 minutes. Tungsten fibre optics have variable intensity, and for this shot a relatively low setting was used so as not to wash out the colour of the chlorophyll in the leaves, but to obtain a rich, deep colour instead.

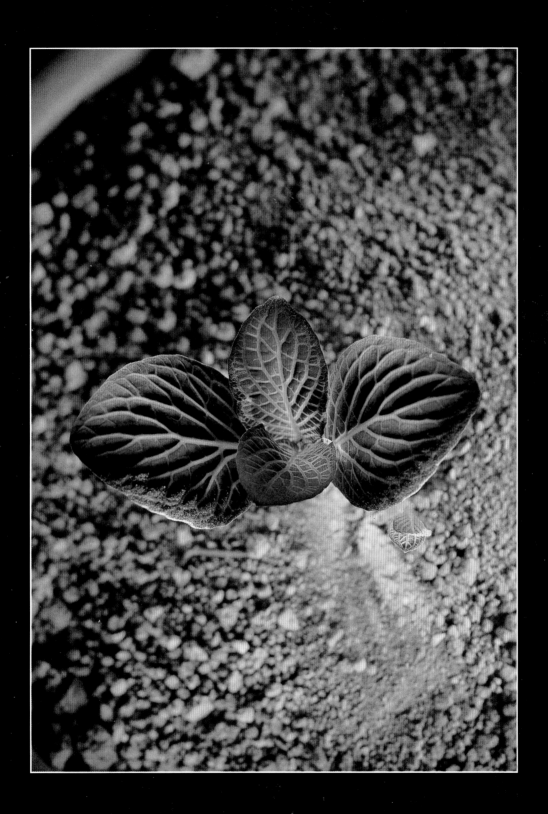

AYERS

▼

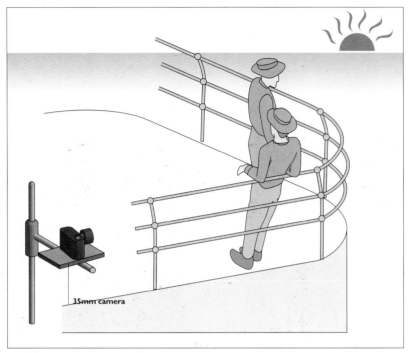

Photographer: **Julia Martinez**

Use: **Portfolio work**

Camera: **Canon EOS 600**

Lens: **300mm**

Film: **Kodak 100**

Exposure: **f/11**

Lighting: **Available light**

► *The original print was colour photocopied and worked in with colour markers to achieve this effect*

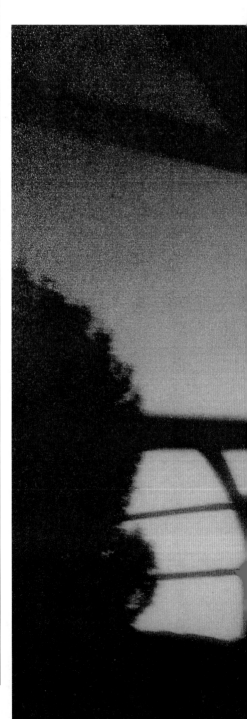

MOODY SILHOUETTED SUNSET SHOTS ARE ALWAYS POPULAR, BUT TO AVOID CLICHÉD FAMILIARITY THE TRICK IS TO COMPOSE SOMETHING WITH BOLD, UNUSUAL FORMS THAT REALLY CATCH THE EYE AND TO CHOOSE A SETTING THAT WILL FIRE THE IMAGINATION.

This is a classic case of choosing just the right moment and capturing it. The sky colour is at just the right point; the highlights on the rails give the perfect definition to the nearside of the silhouetted figures to hint at their embrace. Even the shape of the wide-brimmed hats add to the overall impact of the silhouettes and their angle indicates the inclination of two heads towards each other. Most importantly of all, the railing of the boat adds an unexpected graphic element as well as providing a touchstone clue for the context of the setting; a romantic scene indeed.

Literally, this couple are sailing off into the sunset. Need we say more?

► Good composition is not necessarily always contrived. Take the time to look at the world around you and develop an eye for a strongly composed "candid" shot

► A 300mm lens is useful for longer-range work; the perfect tool for candid shots that won't disturb the subject

► As a rule of thumb, the shutter speed is generally twice the focal length. With longer lenses this length of exposure can become a problem for candid shots, since longer lenses are difficult to hand-hold steadily. Carrying a monopod may be the lightest and most convenient solution for informal or unplanned sessions

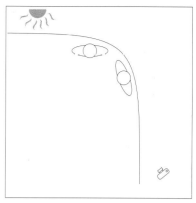

Plan View

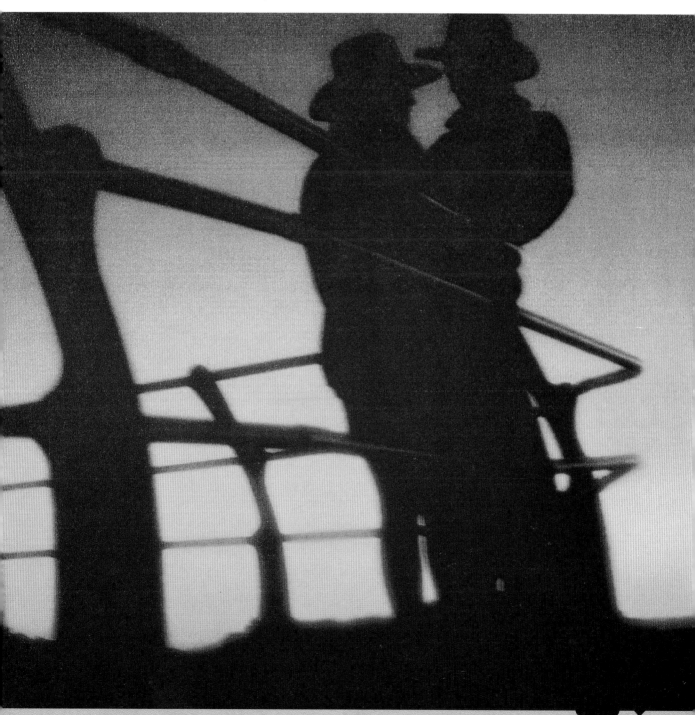

EXPLOSION

▼

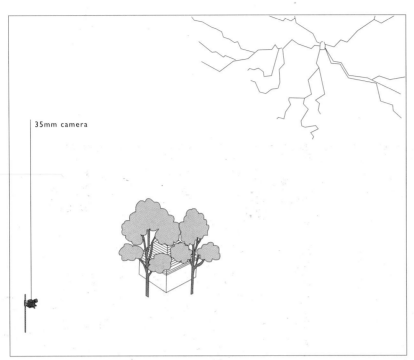

35mm camera

Photographer: **Michael Bath**

Client: **Personal work**

Use: **Editorial, Web page**

Camera: **35mm**

Lens: **50mm**

Film: **Kodak Pro Gold 100**

Exposure: **30 seconds at f/1.8**

Lighting: **Available light (lightning)**

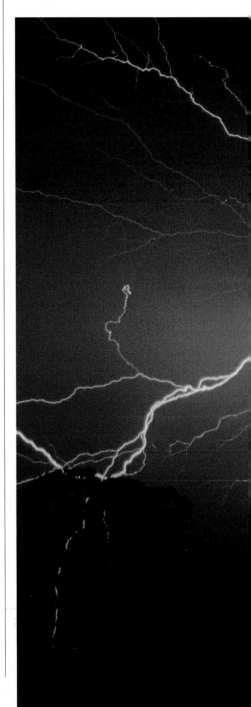

AMAZINGLY, THIS PICTURE IS NOT A MULTIPLE EXPOSURE BUT IS A SHOT OF JUST ONE SINGLE SPECTACULAR BOLT OF LIGHTNING. IT WAS A FLASH WHICH OCCURRED DURING A STORM WHERE THE LIGHTNING STRIKES WERE INFREQUENT BUT GENERALLY OCCURRING ALL IN ONE DIRECTION AND WERE GENERALLY VERY LONG-LASTING.

This meant that Michael Bath was able to set the camera pointing in the right direction on a tripod, and then simply wait for the moment and press the shutter as he saw the flash.

In order to record some foreground colour from the ambient street lights, he then held the shutter open for a further 30 seconds.

The strong composition is well judged, making the most of the natural features of the landscape in conjunction with the unpredictable lightning element. The streaks of lightning behind the trees add to the interest as bolts and branches are entwined, and the fortuitous flashes heading up to the corners of the frame could hardly have been better directed for balance and impact, even if such a thing were possible.

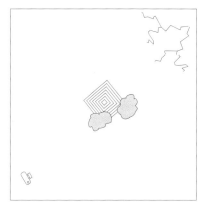

Plan View

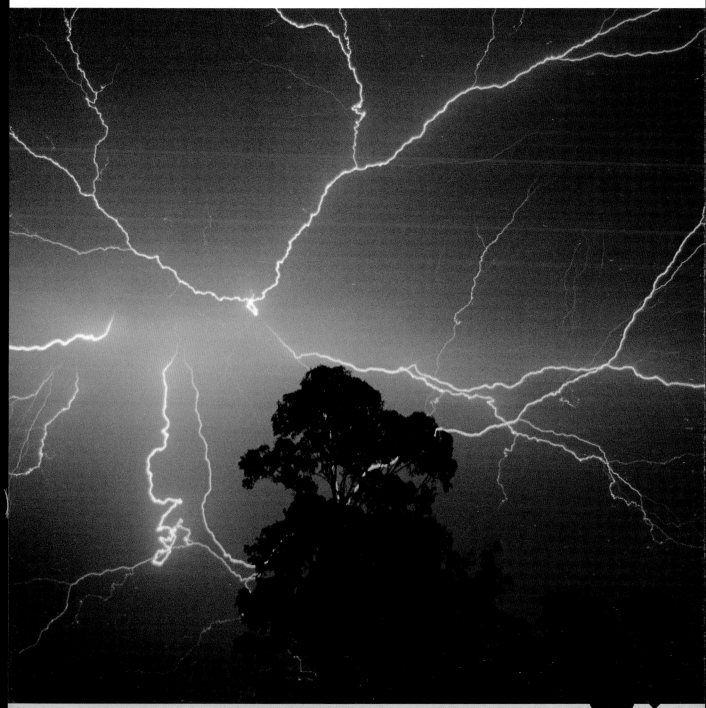

Photographer: **Bob Coates**

Use: **Stock**

Camera: **35mm**

Lens: **35–135mm set at approximately 50mm**

Film: **Fuji Velvia 50**

Exposure: **30 seconds at f/16**

Lighting: **"Black" light**

Props and background: **Black velvet background, mirror base**

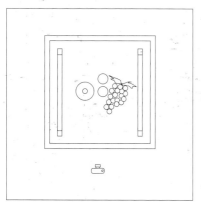

Plan View

C H A M P A G N E

▼

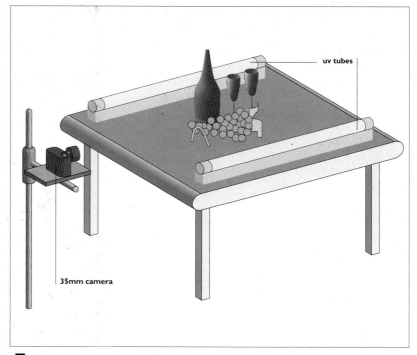

uv tubes

35mm camera

THIS SURREAL EFFECT IS NOT, AS IT MIGHT AT FIRST APPEAR, A COMPUTER-GENERATED IMAGE. THE "SPECIAL EFFECT" IS IN FACT A RELATIVELY STRAIGHTFORWARD TECHNIQUE: FLUORESCENT PAINT ILLUMINATED BY ULTRA-VIOLET LIGHTING.

Bob Coates first painted the items white, then gave them several layers of fluorescent spray paint. The objects were placed on a mirror base, with a black velvet fabric background behind.

The ultra-violet light was provided by two 60cm 18-Watt fluorescent tubes (that is, ultra-violet black light, rather than everyday domestic fluorescent strip lights) laid on either side of the still life, giving the extraordinary characteristic glow-in-the dark fluorescent look.

After experimenting with various combinations of exposure and aperture Bob Coates arrived at an aperture of f/16 which gave him a length of exposure that he was satisfied with at 30 seconds.

► Black (UV) light is wavelengths shorter than about 400nm. Shots in the near ultra-violet are possible with most standard lenses down to about 320nm and most films are sensitive to this. They will record it as a very deep violet

► Beyond 320nm UV light is absorbed by glass and quartz lenses are required

► Reflections in glass can look less intense than the actual object and this can be compensated for (where the composition is suitable) by using a split neutral density filter

Photographer's comment:

Objects painted white first then with fluorescent paint. Bracket for different looks. Take away lights for heavily modelled look. Apply paint in light coats to avoid drips, runs and cracks.

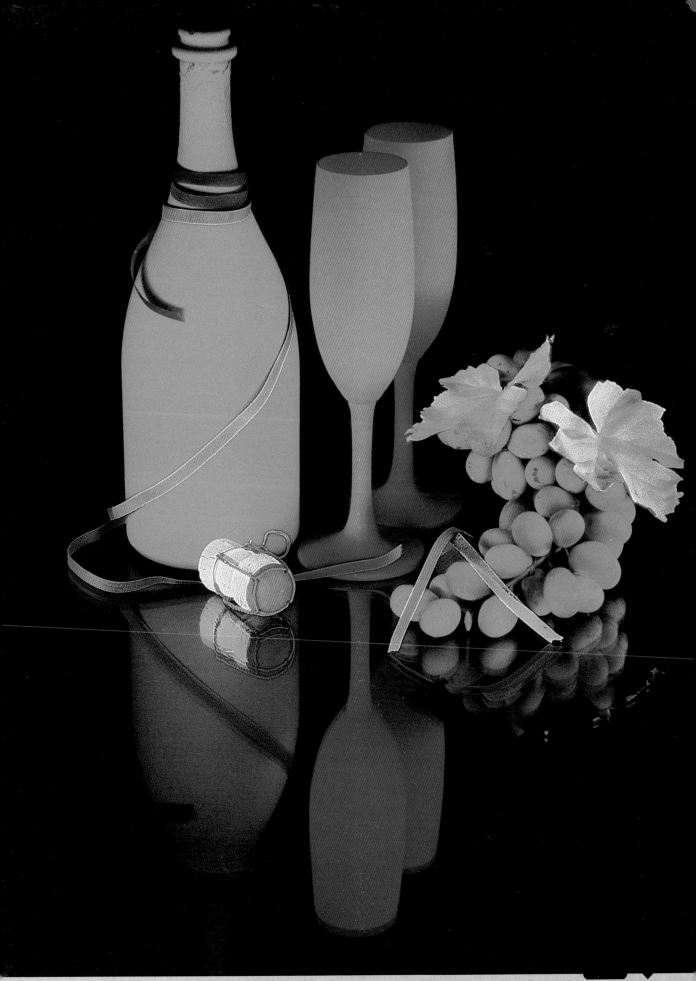

Photographer: **Bob Coates**

Client: **Stock**

Use: **Magazine, brochure, stock**

Models: **Denise Lent, Bob Coates**

Camera: **35mm**

Lens: **35–135mm set at 35mm**

Film: **Fuji RVP 50 EI40**

Exposure: **1/125 second at f/8**

Lighting: **Available light**

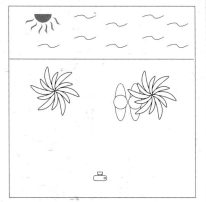

Plan View

BLUEBEARD'S BEACH

▼

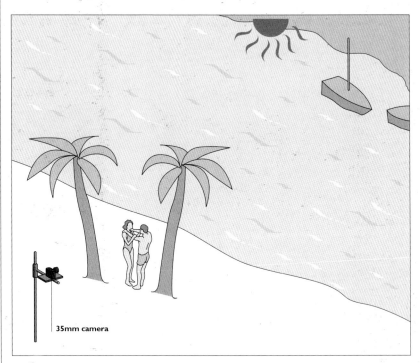

35mm camera

SOMETIMES PRACTICALITIES OF THE SHOOT ON THE DAY WILL DETERMINE THE WAY THE SESSION EVOLVES IN PRACTICE, HOWEVER THE ORIGINAL PLAN MAY HAVE BEEN DEVISED.

On this shoot, Bob Coates's male model didn't make it to the session, so Bob had to improvise and decided to use a timer on the camera to allow for him to run into the frame himself for the shot.

Timing was of the essence as the position of the sun changes very quickly at this time of day, and the composition required it to be in place behind the left palm tree to give the balanced glow of light on either side of the trunk (and to avoid flare in the camera lens). The resulting shot has all the idyllic components of the archetypal romantic image of a paradisical tropical beach at sunset, complete with palm trees, sand and sea.

► *A last-minute change of plan can of necessity inspire a totally different approach from what was originally envisaged*

► *A controlled amount of flare can add to the atmosphere in some contexts*

Photographer's comment:

Meter the sky a little way from the sun in order to create dark silhouettes.

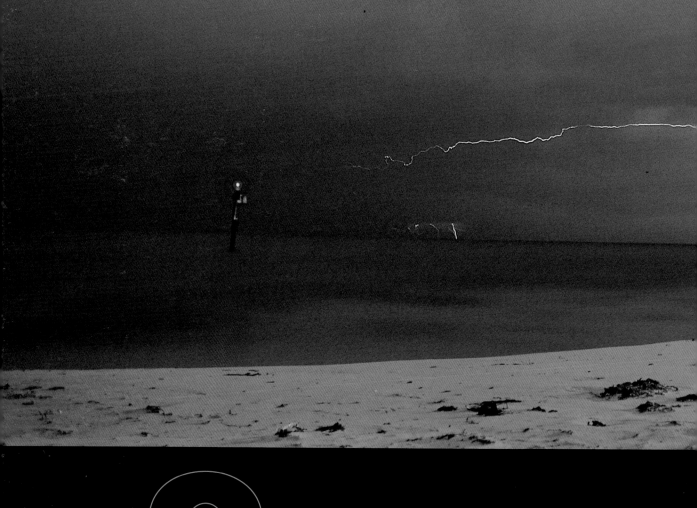

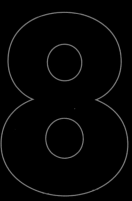

directory of photographers

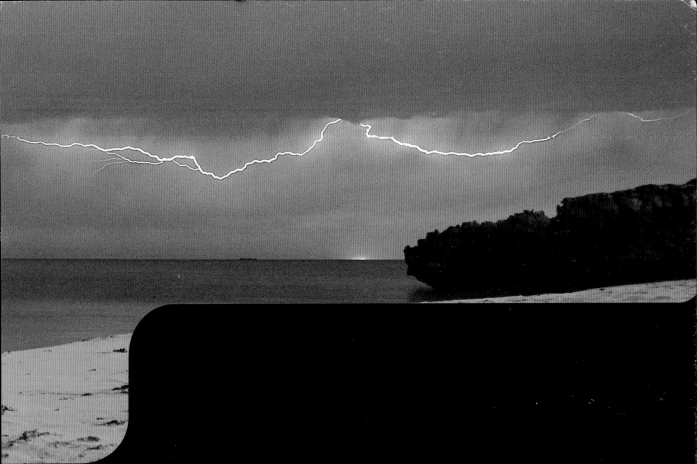

Photographer: MICHAEL BATH

Address: P.O Box 478
BALLINA NSW 2478
AUSTRALIA
Telephone: +61 (0)2 9625 9700
Fax: +61 (0)2 9625 9700
e-mail: mbath@penman.es.mq.edu.au
URL: http://www.ozemail.com.au/~mbath/
Biography: I've had an interest in the weather for many years, in particular thunderstorms. In the mid-1980s I started weather photography, experimenting with sunsets, thunderstorm features and lightning. Although sometimes difficult to get good results, weather photography can be very rewarding. Many of my images are available on the Internet, some of which have been used in newspapers, magazines and calendars.

Night Shots: pp98-99, 148-149

Photographer: BAUER

Studio: BAUER FOTOGRAFIA E PRODUÁ·O LTDA
Address: AV. DEP. EMILIO CARLOS, 1247
02721-100 SAO PAULO
SP – BRAZIL
Telephone: +55 11 858 4338
Fax: +55 11 858 4338
Biography: *Bauer is 42 years old and has been working as a professional photographer since 1987. Initially from a marketing career, he became a photographer because of his deep passion for images. He works in different fields: fashion, beauty, advertising and still life, and his photos are usually recognised by his natural ability for taking a sensual and refined approach. Sensuality is a personal concern of his and a regular characteristic of his work. There is a simple explanation for his peculiar point of view: the natural beauty and sensuality that he sees in the Brazilian people.*

Night Shot: p143

Photographer: BENEDICT CAMPBELL

Address: THE FOUNDRY
WILSHAM ROAD
ABINGDON
OXFORDSHIRE OX14 5HP
ENGLAND
Telephone: +44 (1235) 533288
Fax: +44 (1235) 533290
Biography: *I began my career in photography aged 17 years. I never went to college. Thirteen years on I still spend as much time as possible experimenting and for that reason my clients come to me for*

new looks. I am also a painter so I can look at photography from a different angle – that is,. pure imagery. As clichéd as it might be, light is truly magical and has been my inspiration from the beginning.

Night Shot: p19

Photographer: GUIDO PATERNÒ CASTELLO

Studio: GPS STUDIA LTDA
Address 1: AVENIDA HENRIQUE DODSWORTH 83/1005
COPACABANA
RIO DE JANEIRO
BRAZIL
Address 2: AVENIDA HENRIQUE DUMONT 53/301 COB.
IPAMENA
RIO DE JANEIRO
BRAZIL
Telephone: +55 (21) 287 0789
Fax: +55 (21) 521 8064
Biography: *Born in New York, 19 March 1958, Associate Arts degree at the American College in Paris, June 1979. BA in Industrial and Scientific Photographic Technology at Brooks Institute of Photographic Arts and Science, June 1984. His clients are all major agencies based in Rio de Janeiro. He has won various awards including a silver medal in 1992, gold medal in 1993, bronze medals in 1994 and 1995 from ABRACOM (Brazilian Association of Marketing and Advertising).*

Night Shots: pp41, 110-111

Photographer: BOB COATES

Studio: BOB COATES PHOTOGRAPHY
Address: 6501 RED HOOK PLAZA SUITE 201
ST THOMAS USVI 00802 1306
Telephone: +1 (809) 777 8426
e-mail: bcphoto@islands.vi
URL: http://www.usvi.net/cobox/people/bob
Biography: *St Thomas-based Caribbean photographer Bob Coates is available for assignments from location to studio productions. In addition to having his own business, he also shoots for the local newspapers, is a stringer for the Associated Press and illustrates articles for the magazine writer Joan Amerling. Bob was selected by the Virgin Islands Council on the Arts to photograph the work of territory artists. His photography is exhibited regularly in more than half-a-dozen restaurants on St Thomas and his images are frequently seen in many of*

the island-related publications and tourism brochures.
He is represented by Index Stock Photography.

Night Shots: pp59, 151, 153

Photographer: NICK DJORDJEVIC

Studio: GENESIS FINE ART PHOTOGRAPHY
Address: PO BOX 186
NORTH BEACH
WA 6020
AUSTRALIA
Telephone: +61 (8) 9401 2218
Fax: +61 (8) 9401 5000
E-mail: nick@genesisfineart.com.au
URL: http://www.genesisfineart.com.au
Biography: *Nick Djordjevic is a lightning, coastal landscape and underwater photographer who turned to photography after the onset of chronic arthritis forced him to give up work. He is an acclaimed professional fine art photographer and has produced a series of high-quality fine art lithographic poster prints, 'The Fire from the Sky Collection', together with a series of limited edition landscape, underwater and lightning photographs. These are available to view and purchase at his Web site. Nick is an Associate Member of the Australian Institute of Professional Photographers (AIPP) and is a member of the Society of Advertising, Commercial and Magazine Photographers. His work was also accepted for inclusion in the 1996 editions of Design Down Under 4 and the Society of Advertising, Commercial and Magazine Photographers (ACMP) Collection No. 3.*

Night Shots: pp68-69, 70-71, 72-73, 82-83, 88-89, 94-95

Photographer: EMMA FRATER

Address: STONEVILLE
114 TROWBRIDGE ROAD
HILPERTON
WILTSHIRE BA14 7QG
ENGLAND
Telephone: +44 (0) 1225 765397
Fax: +44 (0) 1225 765397
Biography: *Born in 1969, my parents gave me a Box Brownie camera when I was 5 years*

old and I've been taking photographs ever since. I've recently returned to live in the UK after living in Australia. I studied Fine Art in Perth, Western Australia, before transferring to the University of Technology, Sydney, where I trained for 4 years as a Visual Communicator. After working as a graphic designer for 3 years, I'm now enjoying photographic freelancing. My specialities are environmental portraits and landscapes in colour and black and white, with toning and hand colouring.

Night Shot: p132-133

Photographer:	**WOLFGANG FREITHOF**
Studio:	WOLFGANG FREITHOF STUDIO
Address:	342 WEST 89TH STREET #3
	NEW YORK
	NY 1002Y
	USA
Telephone:	+1 212 724 1790
Fax:	+1 212 580 2498
Biography:	New York-based freelance photographer with international clientele spanning a wide range of assignments from fashion, advertising, editorial, record covers to portraits, as well as fine art for gallery shows.

Night Shot: pp33

Photographer:	**STEWART GOLDSTEIN**
Studio:	EYE CATCHERS PRESS
Address:	THE COACH HOUSE
	CANNON HILL
	LONDON N14 7GH
	ENGLAND
Telephone:	+44 (0) 181 886 0101
Fax:	+44 (0) 181 886 5060
Biography:	Business and Industry Photographer of the Year 1994; Business and Industry Special Award for Excellence 1995; Guinness Black and White Award for Best Picture 1996. Specialise in press and corporate photography.

Night Shot: p43

Photographers:	**TONY AND DAPHNE HALLAS**
Address:	165 ALTO DRIVE
	OAKVIEW, CA 93022
	USA
Telephone:	1 (805) 650 6562
E-mail:	ahallas@west.net
URL:	www.west.net/~ahallas

Agent:	MICHAEL MARTIN
Address:	SCIENCE PHOTO LIBRARY
	LONDON
Telephone:	+44 (0) 171 727 4712
Biography:	(Tony) I have worked in the field of colour photography for almost 30 years. I have a Professional Bachelor of Arts Degree from Brooks Institute, and I did my apprenticeship with Alto Davis at Thomson Photo Lab in Coral Gables. In 1978 I founded Hallas Photo Lab in Ventura County, California which has grown to be a successful business. I have been active in astrophotography for ten years and have been published all over the world. I am a contributing photographer to Sky and Telescope magazine. Represented by Michael Martin at Science Photo Library in London. Clients include Disneyland, Disneyworld, Disney Imagineering, Newsweek and all the major astronomy magazines.

Night Shots: pp60-61, 64-65

Photographer:	**TIM HAWKINS**
Address:	35 NANSEN ROAD
	LONDON SW11 5NS
	ENGLAND
Telephone:	+44 (0) 171 223 9094
Fax:	+44 (0) 171 924 2972
Mobile:	+44 (0) 836 586999
Biography:	Ante photography: Digger driver, Fleet Air Arm helicopter pilot, J. Walter Thompson and more. First photographic commission: lady holding cup of tea, Uxbridge, 1981, fee £22.50 including materials. Worst moment: arriving on location with no lens for 4x5 inch camera. Training: "Uncle" Colin (Glanfield), Plough Studios, London. Good at: orange segments to Landscape Arch and interiors.
Work/work:	Glaxo, Philips, Observer, TSB, Royal Navy, Independent, Lancome, Prince Waterhouse, Trafalgar House, P&O.
Work/play:	Books – Photographers' Britain, Dorset (1991), WWII American Uniforms (1993). Best purchase: Linhof Technikardan. Favourite camera: Leica M2 +21mm. Photographers that come to mind: Strand, Coburn, Brandt, Brassai, George Rogers, Capa, Larry Burrows, Tim Page. Outlook: CC20R + CC05M.

Night Shots: pp44-45, 48-49, 74-75, 96-97

Photographer:	**AGELOU IOANNIS**
Studio:	A1 – PHOTOGRAPHER
Address:	20 XATZILAZAROU STREET 546.43
	THESSALONIKI
	GREECE
Mail:	PO BOX 50797 - 54014
	THESSALONIKI
	GREECE
Telephone:	+30 (0) 31 813 772 (studio)
Pager:	+30 (0) 31 237 400
Fax:	+30 (0) 31 238 854
Biography:	Commercial still life photographer with clients throughout Greece. Teacher of photography and writer as well. Interested in alternative lighting techniques and combinations of different light sources. Involved in digital imaging. Agelou likes to broaden his vision constantly.

Night Shot: p53

Photographer:	**MIKE KÁROLY**
Address:	H-1055 BUDAPEST
	FALK MIKSA UTCA 32
	HUNGARY
Telephone:	+36 (1) 11 21 328
Biography:	Freelance photographer. Member of the Hungarian Arts Foundation and Hungarian Photo Designers Chamber (HPDC).

Night Shots: pp26-27, 39, 84-85, 102-103

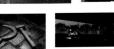

Photographer:	**TAN WEE KHIANG**
Studio:	PHOTO-IMPRESSIONS PTE LTD
Address:	275 THOMSON ROAD
	#02-03 NOVENA VILLE
	SINGAPORE 307645
Telephone:	+65 254 7677

Night Shot: p145

Photographers:	**BEN LAGUNAS AND ALEX KURI**
Studio:	BLAK PRODUCTIONS PHOTOGRAPHERS
Address:	MONTES HIMALAYA 801
	VALLE DON CAMILO
	TOLUCA
	MEXICO CP501 40
Telephone:	+52 (72) 17 06 57
Fax:	+52 (72) 15 90 93

Biography: Ben and Alex studied in the USA and are now based in Mexico. Their photographic company, BLAK Productions, also provides full production services such as casting, scouting, etc. They are master photography instructors for Kodak; their editorial work has appeared in national and international magazines and they also work in fine art with exhibitions and work in galleries. Their work can also be seen in The Golden Guide, the Art Directors' Index and other publications. They work all around the world for a client base which includes advertising agencies, record companies, direct clients and magazines.

Night Shots: pp23, 129

Photographer: **LEWIS LANG**
Address: 83 ROBERTS ROAD
ENGLEWOOD CLIFFS
NJ 07632
USA
Telephone: +1 (201) 567 9622
+1 (201) 568 9682
Agent: SWANSTOCK
118 SOUTH 5TH AVE STE 100
TUCSON, AZ 85701, USA
Telephone: +1 (520) 622 7133
Fax: +1 (520) 622 7180
Biography: *I began my career as a film-maker, making commercials and documentaries for both broadcast and cable TV. Since then I've been both a freelance photojournalist, a fashion photographer and a fine art photographer, working on my own surrealistic narrative, people and still-life photography and have exhibited at numerous fine art galleries across the USA. My fine art photography is also on file with Swanstock, a stock agency that specialises in fine art photography. Both my writing and photography have appeared in Shutterbug, the third largest photo magazine in the world.*

Night Shots: pp21, 31, 121, 135, 140-141

Photographer: **ALEX LARG**
Address: P.O. BOX 1830
BUCKINGHAM MK18 1ZQ
ENGLAND
Telephone: +44 (0) 1280 821023
Mobile: +44 (0) 973 503442
Fax: +44 (0) 1280 821023
Biography: *Background in film, television and photography. Now working in educational fields as well as commercial commissions. Currently exploring digital work for future projects.*

Night Shot: pp54-55

Photographer: **HARRY LOMAX**
Studio: HARRY LOMAX PHOTOGRAPHY
Address: THE ANNEXE
HIGH STREET
HENLEY-IN-ARDEN B95 5AA
ENGLAND
Telephone: +44 (0) 1564 794 001
Fax: +44 (0) 1564 794 752
Biography: *Industrial and commercial photographer specialising in architecture of buildings photography, mainly for leisure sector. Clients tend to be architects or designers who look for a realisation of the atmosphere they are trying to create. Always a user of flash (Bowens Mono heads) for interior. Harry much prefers to let exteriors do their own thing wherever possible but sometimes they do need help with detail.*

Night shots: pp104-105, 106-107, 112-113

Photographer: **PACO MACIAS**
Address: CARRETERA MEXICO TOLUCA #1725
LOCAL A-15
COL. LOMAS DE PALO ALTO
CUAJIMALPA, DF
MEXICO CITY
MEXICO CP 05110
Telephone: +52 (5) 259 9390
+52 (5) 259 9618
Fax: +52 (5) 257 1012
+52 (5) 257 1456
e-mail: fmacias@netmex.com
URL: http://www.pacomacias.com.mx
Biography: *My speciality is photography in advertising and editorial. I'd rather start working with a concept than a layout – in that way I get my best photos. I search, experiment and find the unexpected. This is the most interesting act in the process of creation.*

Layouts – in a personal view – I see as a puzzle of pictures drawn by an art director taken from photo books. This way of work limits creativity in contemporary photography. I have 26 years experience as a professional photographer. My career began as a hobby and I went to a photography school back in 1970 for a one-year course here in Mexico City. I'm 45 years old and run my own studio. I work with 4x5, 6x6 and 35mm formats, on location or in the studio. My preferences are fashion, still life, effects and people. I consider myself a photo-designer.

Night Shot: p29

Photographer: **ANDRÉ MAIER**
Address: 104 SUFFOLK ST #12
NEW YORK
NY 10002
USA
Telephone: +1 (212) 254 3229
Fax: +1 (212) 254 3229
e-mail: maier@artbox73.com
URL: http://www.artbox73.com/maier
Biography: *German photographer André Maier has studied professional photography at the London College of Printing in England and now lives and works in New York City. His diversity in style – from photojournalism and travel photography to conceptual portraiture – has earned him numerous exhibitions in Europe and New York. Through a collaboration with make-up artist Helene Gand, he is now concentrating on expressing creative ideas and concepts through full body make-up, original sets and some computer retouching. His clients include record companies, magazines and ad agencies.*

Night Shots: pp76-77, 127

Photographer: **JULIA MARTINEZ**
Studio: VIVA PHOTOGRAPHY
Address: GLOUCESTERSHIRE GL50 2NG
ENGLAND
Telephone: +44 (0) 1242 237914
Fax: +44 (0) 1242 252462
Biography: *Since Completing her photography degree and being sponsored by Kodak, Julia has launched her own photographic business, Viva Photography. She specialises in model portfolio shots, portraits and beauty photography commissions and has renewed her own career as a model, shooting her own model portfolio in the*

process! Julia now combines a career in front of and behind the lens, which makes life very confusing but always enlightening! She can be contacted for photographic commissions and model work at the number given.
Night Shots: pp131, 146-147

Photographer: **MARTIN MONAGHAN**
Address: BANBRIDGE CO. DOWN
c/o LISBURN HIDE CO LTD
1 DAGGER ROAD
MAZE, LISBURN
CO ANTRIM
NORTHERN IRELAND BT28 2TJ
Telephone: +44 (0) 1846 621381
Fax: +44 (0) 1846 621 920
Biography: *Accountancy background. Self-taught photographer. Martin holds a Fellowship in Contemporary Photography from RPS and is a regular exhibitor.*
Night Shot: pp124-125

Photographer: **PATRICIA NOVOA**
Studio: IMAGO LTDA
Address: GENERAL FLORES 83
SANTIAGO – CHILE
PROVIDENCIA
Telephone: (+02) 251 0025
Fax: (+02) 235 6625
Biography: *Nace in Santiago en 1957. Licenciada en Arte, mencion grabado, en la PUCCh y Fotografa Profesional, Nivel Superior, de la Escuela de Foto Arte de Chile. Ejerce la docencia desde 1982 en el area de grabado en la Escuela de Arte de la PUCCh. Desde 1982 es profesora de fotografia basica y avanzada en los Cursos de Extension de la PUCCh. Ha participado en diversas exposiciones de grabado tanto en Chile como en el extranjero.*
Ademas de la docencia, actualmente realiza su creacion personal en fotografia y es socia de Imago Ltda, empresa privida dedicada al diseno y la fotografia.
Night Shots: p80-81

Photographer: **TIM ORDEN**
Studio: TIM ORDEN PHOTOGRAPHY
Address: POB 1202
KULA, HI 96790
HAWAII
Telephone: +1 (808) 876 0504

Fax: +1 (808) 876 0504
Biography: *Clients ask me, "Where is your studio?" I laugh and tell them that it's the entirety of Hawaii. When I lived in Seattle I had a studio downtown but found myself waiting for the weather to clear so I could shoot outdoors. My ideas come from manifestations of daydreams I've had about how things could look. Maui is my home, Hawaii is my studio. It's funny, just writing about this gets me excited to create some new work.*
Night Shots: pp86-87, 92-93, 123, 138-139

Photographer: **SALVIO PARISI**
Address 1: VIA XX SETTEMBRE 127
20099 SESTO S. GIOVANNI
MILANO
ITALY
Telephone: +39 (2) 22 47 25 59
+39 (2) 48 95 27 16
Address 2: VIA MILISCOLA 2A TRAV. 31
80072 ARCO FELICE
NAPOLI
ITALY
Telephone: +39 (81) 866 3553
Fax: +39 (81) 866 1241
Address 3: VIA SAN CRISOGONO 40
00153 ROMA
ITALY
Telephone: +39 (6) 581 5207
Mobile: +39 336 694739
Biography: *According to the needs of commercial and editorial photography, which is what I mostly work with, I consider it essential for a photographer to always represent the "job-fiction" through his own style and in respect of (i) the main idea of the client and (ii) the philosophy for a product or name and factory. Assuming these as basics, I always tend to refer to a few fundamental "instruments" such as: a planning schedule, technical precision and an overall aesthetic effect – in other words a professional working system.*
Night Shots: pp35, 108-109

Photographer: **CHRIS ROUT**
Address: 9 HEYTHROP DRIVE
ACKLAM
MIDDLESBROUGH
CLEVELAND TS5 8QA
ENGLAND
Telephone: +44 (0) 1642 819774
Mobile: 0374 402675
Biography: *A trained commercial diver at 21, Chris went on to train as an underwater photographer. He progressed into freelance photography 7 years ago. A successful professional photographer specialising in fashion and lifestyle stock photography, he is based in the north-east of England. Chris has his own studio and regularly takes commissions from magazines, advertising and commercial clients.*
Night Shot: p51

Photographer: **MYK SEMENYTSH**
Studio: PHOTOFIT PHOTOGRAPHY
Address: HAIGH PARK
HAIGH AVENUE
STOCKPORT
CHESHIRE SK4 1QR
Telephone: +44 (161) 429 7188
Fax: +44 (161) 429 8037
Biography: *Cut teeth with "In camera effects" without the nerve for retouching. Thankfully someone invented the Mackintosh. Now run a busy commercial studio in Cheshire shooting a variety of items from cars, trucks, room sets, still lifes, etc. Also do creative industrial/ location photography. Currently doing work for Reebok, GPT, Zenica, Pickeneons, ICI, Medeva, Territorial Army.*
Night Shot: p117

Photographer: **GÜNTHER UTTENDORFER**
Studio: PHOTOGRAPHY AND VIDEO
Address: GELIUSTRASSE 9
12203 BERLIN
GERMANY
Telephone: +49 (30) 834 1214
Fax: +49 (30) 834 1214
Biography: *Self-employed for 11 years, now. I moved to Berlin because this city gives me great inspiration. My style of photography nowadays shows my affinity with shooting movies. If I'm shooting girls I always try to get one special side of their character onto the pictures.*
Night Shots: p24-25

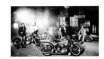

ACKNOWLEDGMENTS

First and foremost, many thanks to the photographers and their assistants who kindly shared their pictures, patiently supplied information and explained secrets, and generously responded with enthusiasm for the project. It would be invidious, not to say impossible, to single out individuals, since all have been unfailingly helpful and professional, and a pleasure to work with.

We should like to thank the manufacturers who supplied the lighting equipment illustrated at the beginning of the book: Photon Beard, Strobex, and Linhof and Professional Sales (importers of Hensel flash) as well as the other manufacturers who support and sponsor many of the photographers in this and other books.
Thanks also to Brian Morris, who devised the Pro-Lighting series, and to Anna Briffa, who eased the way throughout.